BITTER MELON

Inside America's Last Rural Chinese Town

BITTER MELON

Inside America's Last Rural Chinese Town

Jeff Gillenkirk
James Motlow

Introduction by Sucheng Chan

HEYDAY BOOKS
Berkeley, California

Copyright © 1987, 1993, 1997 by Jeff Gillenkirk and
  James Motlow
Calligraphy copyright © 1987 by Angela Chen
Published 1987. Fifth Edition, 2006

Designed by Judy Petry
Composition by University of Washington Deparment
of Printing, Seattle
Printing and binding in Singapore by Imago
Productions

All photographs not otherwise attributed are by James
Motlow.

Jacket photo: *Bing Fai Chow on his porch above Main Street,
Locke, 1976*
Title page photo: *Main Street, Locke, 1984*

LIBRARY OF CONGRESS CATALOGING–IN–PUBLICATION DATA

Gillenkirk, Jeff
Bitter melon
  Bibliography: p.
  1. Chinese Americans—California—Locke—History.
2. Locke (Calif.)—History. I. Motlow, James.
II. Title.
F869.L67G55 1987 979.4'53 87–10418
ISBN 978-0-930588-58-8

Heyday Books
P.O. Box 9145
Berkeley, CA 94709
Tel. (510) 549-3564, Fax. (510) 549-1889
heyday@heydaybooks.com

中
六

念紀開校學民國居樂省洲加美

Main Street, Locke, 1926. *The opening of the Locke Chinese School. (Sacramento River Delta Historical Society)*

Don't marry your daughter to a Gold Mountain Boy
He will not be in bed one full year out of ten
Spiders spin webs on top of her bed
While dust covers fully one side.

—ANONYMOUS

Contents

Preface

MY FATHER FIRST introduced me to the Sacramento Delta in the 1950s, taking me on Sunday drives south from the city along the tree-lined levee roads. Later, as a young man, when the streets of Sacramento were melting and my spirits feeling trapped, I would escape alone down River Road, where the air was softly blowing across the wide, green-yellow fields. From the road atop the levees I could glimpse the slow green river on its way to San Francisco, and stopping my car, I would get out and let the air wrap itself around my body, setting my captured emotions free. I experienced a soundness and a sense of place in the Delta I never felt in Sacramento. I feel the same way today about this remarkable place.

But it wasn't until February 1971 that I became a part of the Delta, when I stopped to visit a friend in Locke on my way to San Francisco. To my surprise, he was planning on leaving, and offered me his place on Main Street to rent. I'd been looking for a place in the country for a long time—for a home away from Sacramento and its white-bread, middle-American culture. I was looking for a refuge, a retreat, a place to study and practice my photography.

Why not Locke? I thought. It was small, quiet, unique; with its Main Street of ramshackle wooden buildings and second-story balconies sloping over the sidewalk, it seemed like a quintessential Hollywood western town, just twenty-five miles from Sacramento. Besides, I'd always wanted to live on Main Street somewhere, for all the sentimental feelings the name connotes. So on a whim, an instinct, I rented his place that day. It was a decision that would affect my life right up to the present day.

My new home was in the bottom floor of a two-story wooden building on Main Street, in what used to be a Chinese restaurant called Happy's Cafe. I spent most of my first winter next to the oven staying warm, writing, thinking, looking for a sense of self. It wasn't long, however, before I discovered that I was one of only three or four non-Chinese living in Locke. My neighbors, men and women, were mostly retired farmworkers who had come to America to earn their fortune, and now were living out their days in this remnant of a rural Chinese culture that once stretched the length of the West Coast. That spring, in fact, a bronze plaque was hammered to the side of the Tules restaurant, commemorating Locke's survival as an all-Chinese town with placement on the National Register of Historic Places.

Here, the awards and articles said, was the last surviving Chinese town built by Chinese, for Chinese, arisen from the ashes of fires that

Railroad workers, Monterey Peninsula, California, 1889. Chinese first came to California for gold, but were driven from the fields by foreign labor taxes and violence. By 1854, as many as a thousand Chinese a month were streaming into West Coast ports, recruited as "coolies" (from the Hindu kuli—*"unskilled laborer"—or more appropriately in Chinese,* k'u-li—*"bitter strength"), for western railroad work. Chinese eventually comprised almost 90 percent of the workforce on the Central Pacific Railroad, working for less than a dollar a day. After the railroads were completed, thousands went to work building the first levees in the Sacramento–San Joaquin Delta, for wages as low as ten cents per cubic yard of earth moved. By 1877, the value of their labor on railroads and land reclamation was estimated by a California land surveyor at nearly $300 million. (California State Library)*

destroyed nearby Walnut Grove's Chinatown in 1915. Here, during Locke's heyday in the 1920s, 1930s, and 1940s, was an autonomous island of Chinese culture, with a permanent population of 600, a seasonal farm labor population of a thousand more . . . with four restaurants, a half dozen markets, dry goods stores, five whorehouses (all staffed by white women), a post office, two slaughterhouses, a flour mill, canneries, shipping wharves, an opera, speakeasies during Prohibition, and the Main Event— as many as five gambling houses operating at once.

Locke was a town like no other, a wide-open *Chinese* western town. And as a non-Chinese living there, I wasn't accepted right away. Out on Main Street, I found my neighbors would pass me by with the same cold avoidance they showed to other whites. I found myself caught between a culture I did not accept, and one that seemed unwilling to accept me. Which was all right with me. Being in the country, in a small town and on my own, was right where I wanted to be. I was twenty-two years old.

After my second winter in Locke I moved back to Key Street, or Second Street—there being only two streets in town—and my relationship with the town began to change. I would sit out on the porch of my house and watch, amazed by almost everything I saw: their town, so small, so poor, yet so orderly beneath a collapsing facade. I remember the exotic peacefulness of seeing almost the entire Chinese population of Key Street parading off to their gardens at dawn, or out to the sloughs to go fishing . . . the women clad in black pajama-like cottons and broad Chinese hats . . . the men in khaki pants and blue work shirts and straw hats . . . all carrying metal buckets and bamboo poles, with burlap bags slung over their shoulders. They all seemed so close to the earth. I learned later that most of them had been tilling the land and fishing since childhood, here and in China's Pearl River Delta. Their gardens here, begun in the 1930s,

teemed with produce year around, probably because I never saw anyone take a thing from the earth without returning some organic matter. This economy seemed to apply to their entire life. It was a way of life—a cleanness, simpleness, and directness—that would profoundly affect my own life and way of seeing things.

Back on Key Street I had my own garden, and I made it a point every morning to wave hello to my neighbors. I usually received a nod, sometimes a wave in return, though little more. Certainly I made no attempt to photograph them at this time. I didn't feel close enough or accepted enough even to ask them for that privilege. Instead, I began exploring and photographing subjects in the Delta and California's nearby Central Valley, pursuing my main photographic interest of people and places— how they fit together, or how they didn't. I studied roadside cafes opened in the forties and fifties, with their chipped, faded neon, their lonely coffee sippers and bored, tired waitresses, the old jukeboxes and scratched, heavy plates; Mexican, Filipino, and Chicano farmworkers, just as I found them in their towns and labor camps; the hot, fertile landscape of the Sacramento–San Joaquin Delta, and the stoic hands who worked it. And every night I returned home to my little house in the peaceful town by the river.

Then one morning that summer my life in Locke changed for good when my most diminutive neighbor, Mrs. Leong, stopped me in the street. In extremely difficult English she asked me to follow her, and led me into the apartment she rented out behind her house. Even more surprising, she led me into the bathroom, which was in very bad shape—the toilet bowl was sinking through a rotting wooden floor. This was the first time in two years I'd ever been invited into a household in Locke. She asked me if I was able to fix it, and of course I said yes, though I didn't know exactly what was in store for me.

It took me more than a week to replace the rotten wood in the floor, the toilet, and the broken plumbing. For compensation, Mrs. Leong fixed dinner for me almost every night that week. Even though she spoke hardly any English and I no Chinese whatsoever, we were able to communicate with gestures, facial expressions, intuition, and laughter. I usually brought my camera with me, and continually asked her and her husband if I could take their pictures. These shy, elderly, Chinese-born farmworkers always refused.

Until one afternoon several months after I'd finished repairing Mrs. Leong's bathroom, I was returning home with a bunch of roses I'd picked for someone, and found her talking with a friend on her front porch; I spontaneously handed the roses to Mrs. Leong, an act which instantly pleased her. She smiled broadly—then pointed to my camera and asked me if I wanted to take her picture. Of course I did! This was the first cooperative portrait I ever took of any of my neighbors in Locke.

My experience with Mrs. Leong—working for her, sharing meals, and her agreement to be photographed—carried me across some kind of invisible barrier with the other townspeople as well. Over the next several months other neighbors agreed to be photographed. I had my camera in hand whenever I left the house, and simply followed my intuition and photographed whatever moved me. I fell in love with this funny, falling-down town and its acres of flowering pear orchards, the confluences of dark river waters at the front and back of town, its gardens and fences and fruit trees, its unusual people. Seventy-five miles upriver from San Francisco, Locke was more like a century away, part of a picturesque agricultural area of winding levee roads and quaint drawbridges, lush Victorian estates and riverfront farm villages hidden among seven rivers crisscrossing the Central Valley between the Coast Range and the Sierra Nevada. The air, the towering skies, the cool summer breezes that blow up from San Francisco Bay, the lush, palpable light of the Delta . . . all these things made the normally blistering valley summers not only livable, but delectable—and eminently photographable. There is a rich, yet subtle, almost silk-like texture to the air among the Delta's thousand miles of silty waterways that is special, even by California standards. No wonder so many of my neighbors chose not to follow their children to the nearby cities, or their ancestors back to China.

Eventually, by popular demand, I became the town's fix-it person, and my willingness to help my elderly neighbors deepened their trust in me. By the following winter I was an accepted citizen of Locke, and so was my camera. For the next eight years I lived and worked there, happily able to share with my neighbors and others the wonder, warmth, and magic I felt about the town, its people, and the simple way of life there through my photographs.

Then in 1979, I moved to San Francisco. I began to see dozens of stories about the history of Locke. Except for one, *American Chinatown,* a 30-minute film by Todd Carrel, none of them ever dealt specifically with the people who lived there, how they got there, and how they lived their lives. After all, if Locke were a nationally historic town, then all of my friends and neighbors—Bing Fai Chow, Mrs. Leong, Wong Yow, Jo Lung, Suen Sum, So Yung, the whole crowd—were Nationally Historic people! I soon realized that not enough of the real story of Locke was being told, because no one had had the opportunity to become a part of the community. But I had. I had many long-standing friendships with my Chinese neighbors, and hundreds of photographs of the town and its people. It was *my* responsibility, I realized, to tell the story of my neighbors' lives in the Golden Mountain—and quickly.

Because the Locke I moved into in 1971 is quickly vanishing. Most of the remaining Chinese are old, and as they die, none are arriving to take their places. Their sons and daughters have gone off to the cities and universities, fleeing the farm laborer's life and leaving Locke's fate to a Hong Kong developer named Ng Tor Tai, who bought the entire town and 450 surrounding acres in 1977 and immediately proposed developing a subdivision of 238 condominia, a yacht marina, and a Chinese "theme park" in the garden area in back. While new county zoning ordinances quickly rendered that plan obsolete, new ones are being proposed continually. Under all of them it seems clear that Locke would cease to be a Chinese community, and become the museum of one instead; it therefore became extremely important to me that Locke's story be told— but by the people who lived it, as personal testimony to the portraits they've allowed me to keep.

In the spring of 1983, after trying unsuccessfully for several years to sell my idea to publishers, I asked friend and professional writer Jeff Gillenkirk to help me organize a book encompassing my photographs and oral histories with the people of Locke. Thankfully he shared my enthusiasm, and jumped head first into the project. As neither of us spoke Chinese, we approached Connie Chan, a bright, cheerful young woman who had grown up in Locke, and hired her as interpreter/translator for those residents who spoke no English. Her familiarity with the Zhongshan dialect and first-name friendship with her neighbors helped open many doors to us.

That summer and fall nearly every weekend found the three of us in Locke, where my mother, Mary Motlow, now had a home, taping stories of my neighbors' experiences in the Golden Mountain. Connie's translations and interviews done in English were then transcribed by a professional service, and edited that winter by Jeff. Over the next two years we did additional oral histories and extensive follow-up interviewing as the manuscript went through various versions. Jeff, meanwhile, was conducting the historical and factual research that became part of our subjects' introductions, the Afterword, and Appendixes, which he wrote at the project's conclusion in October 1986.

I feel deeply honored to have been given the personal histories—and portraits—of Locke's people for this book. This is what follows. But to best understand how they and their town survived to become the last rural Chinese town in America, it helps first to understand how it all started.

AMONG THE THOUSANDS of Chinese a month streaming into West Coast ports in the mid-nineteenth century were ancestors of many of my neighbors in Locke—grandfathers, fathers, and uncles who had come for the riches and opportunities promised in *Gum Shan*, the Golden Mountain. By the 1880s a majority of farmers and farm laborers in California were Chinese, and Chinese mining camps and fishing villages were spread the length and breadth of Oregon, Washington, and Idaho.

But then came a chapter of American history as shameful as any, and as ignored—the "Driving Out," a contagion of violence in which white mobs burned and plundered Chinese communities throughout the West. Major massacres in Los Angeles (1871), Rock Springs, Wyoming (1885), and Douglas Bar, Oregon (1885), succeeded in driving Chinese from their homes. Also in 1885, in Tacoma, Washington, Chinese workers were herded into railroad boxcars and driven from town. In 1886, residents of Seattle's Chinatown were put onto steamships and shipped to San Francisco. In California, pioneer settlements from Yreka in the north to Redlands in the south were disrupted by the Driving Out. Newspapers of the day in Calaveras and Humboldt counties, Sacramento, Chico, St. Helena, Truckee, Antioch, Calistoga, Modesto, Vacaville, and dozens more California locales all reported violent mob action and arson against Chinese—and no legal retribution.

The Sacramento Delta was one of few western sites where Chinese escaped the violence. Here, among tule marshes and peat bogs and silty waterways, the Chinese carved a niche for themselves, hiring out for as little as ninety cents a day to reclaim the floodlands for agriculture, then developing it into the "Asparagus Capital of the World" and the major source of Bartlett pears it is today. Peaceful, hard-working, and agriculturally savvy, many of these refugees from China's Pearl River Region stayed on as sharecroppers and farm laborers. (A fuller explanation of the Chinese contribution to California's agriculture is provided in the Introduction by historian Sucheng Chan.) Undoubtedly the enormous fortunes made by Delta landowners, canners, and shippers helped soothe intolerance of the Chinese: until World War II, Chinese rarely made more than a dollar a day as laborers and domestic help. Also, the Chinese stayed as much to themselves as possible, living in ramshackle sections of Sacramento River towns from Rio Vista to Courtland, sending the bulk of their meager pay back to China.

As in most of the West, the Delta's Chinese population was made up of two separate groups who had emigrated from neighboring districts in Guangdong Province in southeastern China. One group, from Sze Yap,* settled in the Delta towns of Isleton, Rio Vista, and Walnut Grove. The other, from Zhongshan district (near Macao), settled the Chinatown of Courtland, and shared the Chinatowns of Isleton and Walnut Grove with the Sze Yap. Sze Yap Chinese outnumbered Zhongshan by nearly ten to one. As was the custom, each group organized itself along language, district, or family lines into district associations, called "tongs," in order to help Chinese get into this country, and provide assistance and protection upon their arrival. In Walnut Grove and other Delta Chinatowns, Sze Yap and Zhongshan associations were in constant competition for influence, which sometimes erupted into violence. Though these disturbances were often brief and selective in nature—one tong sending out assassins with hatchets to dispense with a nettlesome rival (from whence the term "hatchet man" has come)—the American press dubbed even minor outbreaks "Tong Wars."

In 1915, both the Zhongshan and Sze Yap sections of Walnut Grove's Chinatown burned to the ground. After years of less than peaceful coexistence, rather than rebuild in Walnut Grove the Zhongshan population moved upriver, where two of their countrymen had already established a saloon, a gambling hall, and a boardinghouse, and built themselves a town on land leased from the family of a landowner named George Locke. (Under terms of California's 1913 Alien Land Act, Chinese were not allowed to own land. The law was not declared unconstitutional until 1952.) The deal between the Lockes and eight representative Zhonghsan merchants was sealed with a handshake, and stipulated that the Lockes would clear nine acres of their pear orchard to make room for a new Chinese town in exchange for five dollars a month land rent for each home, ten dollars a month for commercial buildings. Originally Lockeport, the name was later shortened to Locke. The non-English-speaking Chinese began calling it "Lockee," and still do today.

Locke, then, was born as a refuge not only from white violence, but from rival Chinese groups as well. It was the only all-Chinese town in the Delta, and the first established in the West since the Driving Out. For the next fifty years Locke remained an all-Zhongshan town,

---

* Although we have used *pinyin* transliteration for other Chinese place names, we have retained the traditional transliteration of Sze Yap (*pinyin* Siyi), as this is the spelling and pronunciation used by the people of Locke.

with only one tong—the Jan Ying Association—to represent its people's interests.

The people of Locke today speak with tremendous fondness and pride about the heyday of their town. And no wonder. Here was an entire town speaking the same dialect, sharing similiar memories of Zhongshan, and providing a social network for the farm laborers and families of Chinese tenant farmers and sharecroppers in the rich delta lands. Almost immediately, Locke became the cultural and economic nucleus of their lives in the Golden Mountain. The Jan Ying Association helped bring additional relations into the country, or located "paper" relatives for others wishing to come. Mr. Wong Yow, Mr. Bing Fai Chow, Mrs. Jone Ho Leong, Mr. Jo Lung, and Connie Chan all had relatives who had come before them to America, establishing a network of contacts that paved their way. Most had returned to China with some savings, and stories of the work there was to be had in the Golden Mountain—and work, work, and more work. But the more work the more money, and with money, land and a retirement home could be bought in China. This dream of financial independence, a happy retirement, and honor bestowed upon the family brought many people from China during her time of economic depression and political instability, when there was virtually no opportunity for peasants to improve their lot.

The majority of Locke's first residents were single men, members of the so-called "bachelor" society who planned one day to return to China with their American earnings. For most of the year their homes were in the labor barracks in the fields, where they put in ten-hour days, six days a week for one dollar a day. Their one day off was an opportunity to get to Locke, which served the same function to these farm laborers as Dodge City did to cowpunchers. Rooms were available above the town's storefronts on Main Street or in boardinghouses for five dollars a month. Men like

Wong Yow and Bing Fai Chow would rent a room year-round in Locke, sharing it with another worker who would use it in their absence. For just $2.50 a month they had an eight-by-ten-foot room to store their things in, and a place to sleep during the summer when they slipped into Locke for a day of rest, relaxation, and socializing.

By almost everyone's account, the town was filled with a wild vitality during the twenties and thirties. Here were Zhongshan-run markets, restaurants, boarding houses, dry-good stores, barbershops, pool halls, laundries, and gambling halls. The only white-run businesses were the town's five whorehouses, and several speakeasies during Prohibition. There was no law enforcement in Locke, white or otherwise, nor any formal governmental structure. (Locke remains an unincorporated town today.) While individuals could petition the tong for protection, to arbitrate commercial disputes, or for social matters, each business was expected to provide its own security. More than one rowdy gambler found himself flat on his back on Main Street, the victim of "Charlie" Lee Bing's Kung Fu prowess. Lee Bing's dealers also kept newspaper-covered lead pipes and brass knuckles within reach to discourage roisterous behavior; a buzzer was located on the outside front wall of the building, where a lookout was posted to warn of suspicious strangers, possible robbery attempts, or raids. The town went through significant turbulence in the early twenties, when other tongs in the region attempted to establish footholds in Locke; afterwards, it seems to have settled into a long, graceful period of self-monitored vice and cultural harmony. Only within the last decade have people started locking their doors at night, as Caucasians replace Chinese as the predominant group in town.

Surprisingly, more than the Chinatowns in the Delta, Locke became a place for families. Tommy King, whose own family moved from Walnut Grove in 1928, recalls there being between thirty and forty families in Locke during the Depression era. Some women—many already married to Chinese men here—came from China on the underground railroad, circumventing immigration restrictions through patient application and creative paper work. Others were first-generation American, born in the Chinatowns of Isleton, Courtland, Walnut Grove, or San Francisco, and married by choice or family arrangement (a practice in about half of the Delta's Chinese marriages until 1950 or so) to a man from Locke. This generation more than held its own carrying on the strong Chinese tradition of family. Mrs. Effie Lai had five children. Louise Jang had twelve. Mrs. Leong, Mr. Hoy Kee, Mr. Jo Lung, and Locke's other married people we talked with all raised children in town. To many of them, Locke was an ideal place to raise kids. There was a segregated Oriental school in Walnut Grove (which was finally closed in 1941, and the Chinese and Filipinos integrated with the whites, after the Japanese were put in internment camps), a nonsegregated high school eight miles upriver in Courtland, miles and miles of waterways to swim and fish and row in, and the warm Central Valley climate, tailormade for kids. Also, in 1926, Joe Shoong, founder of the West Coast chain of National Dollar Stores (dry goods and clothing), donated the money to build a Chinese school in Locke for the teaching of Chinese language and culture.

While it might seem strange to think of a small town with three gambling halls, five whorehouses, and several speakeasies as an ideal place to raise children, for them it was. As Tommy King points out, the Chinese are a practical people, and were well aware of the needs of a townful of single men. And to Chinese people—Cantonese at least—gambling is not a vice: it's a recreation. Few of Locke's residents ever referred to gambling with any kind of moral overtone: regret, yes, from those who lost some money, but moral objections, hardly

ever. The gambling houses also served important social functions in town. They were meeting places where the men could read Chinese newspapers, play dominoes, fan-tan or chess, enjoy a cup of tea, or relax by playing Chinese musical instruments. They went there to get their mail and share the latest news from home. And when local farmers came to find workers, the gambling houses served as labor hiring halls as well.

Those who didn't gamble or use the town's speakeasies or whorehouses seemed perfectly accepting of those who did—as long as they were left alone. The physical structure of the town helped. All the businesses, boarding houses, hotels, and the poorhouse (where the indigent and those strung out on opium stayed until they found work) were concentrated along Main Street or the south end of town. Most of Locke's families lived in the single-family, "tongue-and-groove" houses (the wood in vertical, fitted construction rather than overlapping clapboards) back on "Second" Street, or Key Street. There, with access to the gardens and waterway in back, they could raise their children and tend their gardens with only incidental contact with the hurly-burly atmosphere of Main Street.

Life was rarely so neatly segregated, however. Mr. Everett Leong talks about shining shoes outside the back door of the gambling halls when he was six years old, hoping for a lottery winner to emerge with a pair of dusty shoes and a twenty-five cent tip. Mrs. Dale Yee tells about the excitement that surrounded the hourly lottery, and the strings of firecrackers set off on Main Street when a big winner was hit. Some of the town's most respected families, the Lees and the Kings, for example, were involved in the gambling business, and found ways to contribute directly to the community. In a joint venture, the gambling houses once provided a new water well for the town. They also bought much of the equipment used in the language school, made many donations to the

Baptist Mission, and helped to care for indigents.

As an all-Chinese town, Locke was intimidating to most of the neighboring whites. Few visited it—except those interested in gambling, prostitutes, or booze (the almost total lack of newspaper or other archival photographs of Locke attests to the little contact the two cultures had). Once a Chinese left the sanctuary of Locke, things were different. Mr. Bing Fai Chow tells of traveling through rural communities and having stones thrown at him by whites. Mr. Suen Sum recalls going as far as San Jose for work, only to be turned away when the farmer refused to hire Chinese help. Others spoke about the humiliation of having to sleep in barns, of cleaning white people's toilets, of suffering the insults of cannery floorwalkers— all for the dubious privilege of collecting a salary of a dollar a day. Yet for the record, at least, most of my Chinese neighbors refused to make a major case about relations with whites. They are country people—humble, stoic, and content to make their point by the integrity of their lives rather than by bitter words (those who died younger or returned to China might have given less gracious replies, however). Those who had originally entered the country as Paper Sons, with papers falsely identifying them as related to a U.S. citizen, were clearly intimidated by the subject, still fearful half a century later of legal retaliation. Those who never learned English seemed to accept discrimination as a natural consequence of not speaking the language; the ones who did learn English were able to get by providing some service the white society wanted—labor contracting, domestic service, or farm tenancy. In any case, the existence of their all-Chinese town allowed many of them to avoid the question of relations with whites altogether.

Given their harsh working conditions and low pay, discrimination, and the necessity for so many to live as bachelors in the Golden Mountain, people often ask me why so many of the Delta's Chinese stayed. For most, conditions were far worse back in China. Many were cut off from family and home by the seemingly endless cycle of political turmoil and warfare that began with the revolution of 1912, continued through the Japanese invasion and World War II, right up through Mao Zedong's Cultural Revolution in the 1960s. Others lost land, holdings—and hope—after the communist takeover in 1949. But mostly, they were separated from their dreams by the Great Depression and their own poverty. As Bing Fai Chow asks hopelessly, how could you plan to return to China when you were making one dollar a day? If a weekend in San Francisco could drain a worker of several month's wages, a trip to China for most was clearly unthinkable.

But they made the most of it. Those who raised children in "Lockee" practiced incredible frugality, some saving enough money from meager salaries to send as many as five children to college. While seeing their children succeed in the Golden Mountain was a dream deferred, it was a dream nonetheless. Once their children had become enmeshed in the American educational and social structure, their own dreams of ever returning to China receded even further. And besides, they had Locke. They could live out their lives in this little Chinese town on the big, slow river, where their gardens flourished in the moist, peaty soil, where the climate, the light, the air of the rich coastal delta soothed and placated them, and erased, in the slow unfolding of the seasons and the years, the need, if not the yearning, to return where they came from.

Bitter Melon—Ku Gua—is a green, summer vine vegetable shaped like a cucumber, with a rough bumpy skin like a crocodile's. Inside is a pale yellow interior filled with seeds, which when cleaned, yields a moist, bitter meat that is very nourishing. It is an acquired taste. Only after several bites do the taste buds become accepting of the pleasures and nourishment bitter melon has to offer. America must have been like a bitter melon for these Chinese who came here expecting riches, respect, and a triumphant return to their home country, and instead encountered segregation, poverty, and widespread discrimination. Yet they persevered. Indeed, considering the strength of the spirits of those who survived, and the prosperity of their offspring, they have prevailed. They carved their niche in the Golden Mountain. And patiently, perseveringly, they drew nourishment and even happiness from the melon that at first seemed to promise them only bitterness.

And for better or worse, they became Americans.

THANKS TO AUTHOR Jeff Gillenkirk for his inspiration and guiding hand with my Preface. Special thanks to my wife, Karen, to Maria Alaniz, June Braun, Connie Chan, and Todd Carrel for his friendship and help in expanding my knowledge of the people of Locke during the making of his television documentary, *American Chinatown*. Jeff and I deeply regret failing to give Todd Carrel proper credit and acknowledgment in the first printing of this book for his interviews with Ng So Yung and Carol Hall which came from his work on the film *American Chinatown*. We are happy to have this now corrected. We are grateful to the Vanguard Foundation of San Francisco for their financial support in the gathering of oral histories. For their time, encouragement, and expert advice, thanks to Sucheng Chan, Roger Daniels, Ping Lee, Tommy and Connie King, Angela Chen, Wei Chi Poon, Melissa Mytinger, Tom Cole, and Bill Chleboun. Thanks also to my mother, Mary Motlow, for her input and encouragement, and the use of her house in Locke as a base of operations. But my deepest thanks go to the people of Locke. It is my hope that publication of *Bitter Melon* will help the American people gain greater knowledge and understanding of the strength, resourcefulness, and character of California's Chinese pioneers, and greater respect for their descendants living among us today.

James Motlow
Oakland, California

Introduction

The Significance of Locke in Chinese American History

To those responsible for preserving the nation's historical landmarks, what qualified the little town of Locke in the Sacramento Delta of California for inclusion in the registry of national historical places was its unique status as the only village in the United States built and inhabited exclusively by Chinese until recent years, when Caucasians began to move in. (Other Chinatowns in California were simply sections of, or districts in, towns and cities that whites had developed.) However, Locke's true significance lies not in its singularity but in the fact that it is a model of other villages and towns that might have been built in rural California had Chinese laborers not been excluded from the United States after 1882. Locke is the most visible monument to the extraordinary efforts made by the Chinese to develop agriculture in California and establish communities in rural America.

From the late 1850s to the early 1920s, thousands of Chinese farmed actively in every major agricultural region of California except the Imperial Valley, and made a significant contribution to the successful commercial production of many California crops. Their greatest endeavors, however, took place in the Sacramento–San Joaquin Delta, which they helped to reclaim and put under the plow. They cultivated the land for a longer period there than anywhere else in the state; in fact, the Delta is the only place in North America where Chinese farmers have maintained a continuous presence for one and a quarter centuries. It is very likely that had immigration exclusion not cut off the influx of Chinese, and had anti-alien land laws not been passed to prevent them and other Asians declared "ineligible to citizenship" from acquiring agricultural land, they would have established a permanent foothold in other agricultural regions as well, and other villages and towns like Locke would have sprung up to serve their needs.

Chinese first came to California to mine for gold, but they soon became truck gardeners and farmers when they discovered that cultivation of the soil provided a more steady living. Getting provisions to the mines was a major undertaking: Chinese merchants shipped sacks of rice and other imported dried foodstuffs via mule trains to mining camps along the foothills of the Sierra Nevada, while some Chinese miners cultivated patches of vegetables, sweet potatoes, and various kinds of small fruit on their claims. By the early 1860s, Chinese were growing vegetables in virtually every mining camp where they were found, and in towns such as Sacramento, Marysville, Chico, Oroville, Auburn, Nevada City, Grass Valley, Placerville, and Sonora along major transportation routes. Both the merchants and the miners-turned-gardeners found that the profits to be made by provisioning their countrymen were considerable.

Within a decade the Chinese had begun to lease and buy land for farming on a larger scale. On tracts upwards of a hundred acres, they grew a variety of crops, including field crops such as wheat, barley, oats, corn, and alfalfa, though the majority specialized in vegetables. Selling to both Chinese and non-Chinese customers, itinerant peddlers distributed fresh produce on foot and in horse carts. The presence of Chinese farmers growing field crops and deciduous tree fruit was recorded in the 1870 and 1880 U.S. censuses of agriculture, as well as in land leases and crop mortgages in almost all the counties of California.

The most challenging task undertaken by Chinese agricultural pioneers was reclamation of the Sacramento–San Joaquin Delta for farming. Formed by the confluence of California's two major rivers, the Sacramento and the San Joaquin, the Delta is an inverted estuarine marshland that narrows as it approaches the sea. (Normal deltas broaden as they flow seaward.) The inversion results from the fact that the Coast Range contains only a single, narrow break east of the Carquinez Straits through which the waters of both river systems must pass before they reach Suisun and San Francisco bays. Every spring and summer, when the effluence was voluminuous, the waters backed up to flood hundreds of square miles, creating a deltaic swamp. Tall bullrushes, known as tules, grew in this marshland, dying annually and decaying to form a rich organic soil known as peat.

Though farmers soon recognized the fertility of peat soil, they also found that before it could be safely cultivated, levees had to be built to protect the land from floods. Ordinary draught animals could not be used to build the levees, as their hoofs sank in the soft muck. Moreover, white laborers could not be found to reclaim the tule lands, because working conditions in the region were extremely unpleasant and unhealthy. Even after the dikes, drains, and levees had been built, the thickly matted peat sod had to be broken up before it could be plowed. Ordinary plows could not do the job; special implements with sharp knives attached had to be used to cut through the layers of decaying tules. And once the sod was broken up, after several years of cultivation the peat became a dust so fine that it seeped into houses, nostrils, and the pores of skins. Chinese were the only laborers that landowners could find to perform the reclamation work, and later to farm the reclaimed peat. They were the mainstay of the many "wheelbarrow brigades" that reclaimed the Delta before the 1880s; they also comprised the first large group of tenant "tule farmers." After the clamshell dredger—a barge with two large claw-like buckets at the end of a long boom used to scoop out and deposit the fill on the levees—was introduced in 1879, heavy equipment eventually replaced Chinese laborers in reclamation work. Chinese tenant farmers, however, remained dominant until the Japanese overtook them after the turn of the century.

In the late 1860s and early 1870s many Chinese were available for virtually any kind of work, no latter how unpleasant or low paid, as opportunities in mining and railroad construction began to decrease. Though the dream of finding gold persisted among the Chinese long after whites had given it up, by the 1860s placer claims had been exhausted and Chinese miners did not feel secure enough (because white miners relentlessly drove them away from good claims) to invest in expensive machinery to tap the gold beneath the surface. When the first transcontinental railroad—the construction of which had employed over 10,000 Chinese—was completed in 1869, the Central Pacific Railroad Company dismissed thousands of Chinese workers. The railroad's use of them in labor gangs gave other entrepreneurs the idea of employing Chinese in other large construction projects, and swampland reclamation and levee building was one such enterprise.

Individuals such as the pioneer Reuben Kercheval, who settled near Courtland in 1849, and the Dutch immigrant P. J. van Löben Sels, who arrived in the Delta in the mid-1870s, hired dozens of Chinese to build levees for them. But the largest reclamation efforts using Chinese labor were undertaken by George D. Roberts, president of the Tide Land Reclamation Company, established by San Francisco and Oakland capitalists in 1869. Roberts obtained tens of thousands of swampland acres from the state of California through both legal and illegal means. In testimony before a congressional committee in 1876, he estimated that he had used 3,000 to 4,000 Chinese laborers to reclaim 30,000 to 40,000 acres. He arranged with Chinese labor contractors (who were mainly merchants) to hire laborers to build specified lengths of levees. The contractors were paid by the number of cubic yards of fill dug up and piled, and each Chinese laborer made approximately one dollar a day. The average cost of reclamation was seven dollars per acre, and since Roberts paid only two or three dollars to buy each acre of unreclaimed land—and sold the reclaimed tracts for twenty to a hundred dollars per acre—he made a handsome profit.

Chinese began in the late 1860s to lease land for farming in the Delta, where three patterns of leasing emerged. Along the periphery of the Delta which was reclaimed first, Chinese leased portions of tracts located on natural levees around the rims of the islands or on mainland tracts owned by white farmers, who often contracted them to plant fruit trees on the rented acreage. While caring for the saplings, the Chinese were permitted to use the land between the trees to cultivate vegetables. Chinese usually leased no more than forty acres of orchard land in these areas.

A second pattern was found in the depressed centers of the peat islands, in the northern and southern ends of the Delta. Known as backswamps, these tracts were suitable primarily for field crops. Some of the earliest leases Chinese made were for these backswamp tracts, each measuring several hundred acres; in exchange for reclaiming them, they were allowed to hold (and presumably farm) the land without paying rent for one or two years, after which they would pay a modest sum per acre. Most of these tracts were owned by individual landowners, and Chinese tenants grew grain and hay as well as potatoes, onions, beans, and vegetables on them.

A third pattern emerged in the islands of the central Delta, which had no natural levees and were below sea level. This portion of the Delta could be reclaimed only with dredges and other modern equipment. The cost of reclamation was so high that only large corporations could afford to carry out the work. Chinese leased land to grow Irish potatoes from a dozen or more corporations, such as the Middle River Navigation and Canal Company, the Empire Navigation Company, the Venice Island Land Company, and the Rindge Land and Navigation Company, which financed the reclamation of the central Delta. By the turn of the century, the Chinese had become important growers of potatoes in the Delta. The most prominent of them was Chin Lung, the Chinese "Potato King"—a contemporary of George Shima, the Japanese "Potato King." But potato cultivation eventually declined because peat soil develops a fungus when planted to potatoes for more than three straight years.

In the twentieth century, the crop that drew the largest amount of Chinese labor was asparagus. The Delta became the premier asparagus growing region in the world because the fine peat soil enabled the asparagus shoots to grow very straight, which facilitated canning. In the early decades of the twentieth century, Chinese provided the bulk of the labor in both the asparagus fields and canneries of the Delta. The largest cannery in the Delta was owned by an enterprising Chinese, Thomas Foon Chew.

Locke was not built until the Chinese had been engaged in Delta agriculture for half a century. Founded long after the Chinese had

Chinese workers in packing shed. *By 1886, despite passage of the Chinese Exclusion Act (1882), a majority of farm tenants, sharecroppers, and agricultural laborers in California were Chinese. They worked the fields and orchards of the new Delta farmlands, planting, picking, and packing fruit, asparagus, and seeds for shipment around the world. (La Vern Studio/Frank Cowsert)*

secured a foothold in the area, it overnight became a fully developed village with all the services that resident Chinese tenant farmers and migrant farm laborers sought. It was built by a "secessionist" group of immigrants from Zhongshan district in Guangdong province, who had originally settled in the Chinatown of Walnut Grove, one of four Chinatowns situated on the Sacramento River. The other Chinese residents in Walnut Grove came from the neighboring region of Sze Yap, "the Four Districts"—a collective name for Xinhui, Taishan, Kaiping, and Enping districts. When the Walnut Grove Chinatown burned down in 1915,

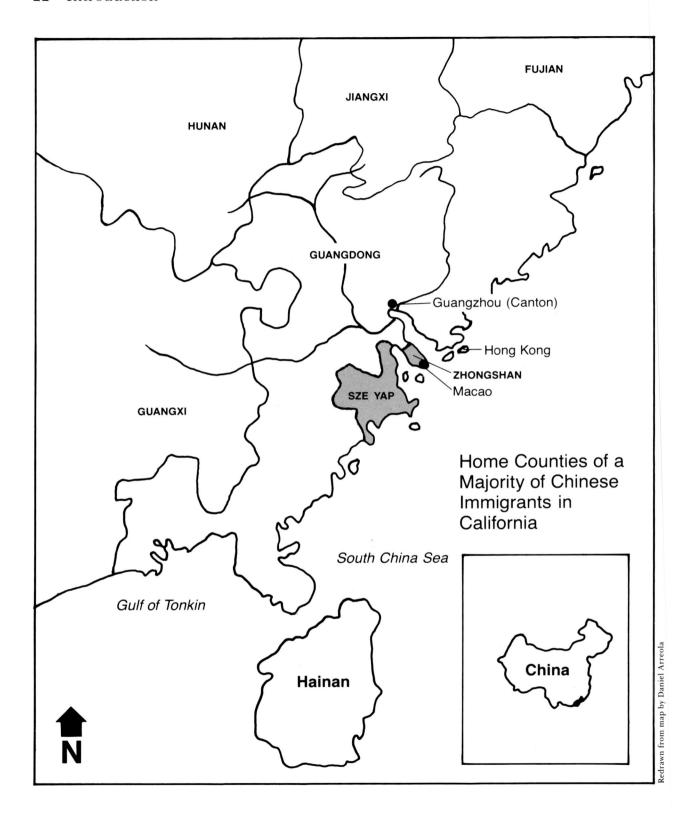

FUJIAN

JIANGXI

HUNAN

GUANGDONG

Guangzhou (Canton)

Hong Kong

ZHONGSHAN

Macao

SZE YAP

GUANGXI

Home Counties of a Majority of Chinese Immigrants in California

South China Sea

Gulf of Tonkin

Hainan

China

N

Redrawn from map by Daniel Arreola

several Zhongshan merchants decided not to join the Sze Yap residents to rebuild it. Their decision reflected age-old social cleavages brought over from their homeland.

Although Zhongshan and Sze Yap are close by, dialects in China are so finely differentiated that people living in adjoining districts who spoke slightly different dialects looked upon their neighbors as virtual foreigners. Chinese emigrants often accentuated such dissimilarities in overseas settlements by sticking to their own dialect group through membership in the same district and/or clan associations, and by following the same occupations. Zhongshan emigrants in the United States specialized in fruit growing and congregated along the natural levees of the northern Sacramento Delta; Sze Yap people tended to go into potato cultivation in the backswamps further south.

Located on a mainland tract along Georgiana Slough across from the northern tips of both Grand and Andrus islands, Walnut Grove sat astride a natural levee that quickly dipped into the backswamps. Residents of the town cultivated a wide variety of crops: fruit, potatoes, onions, beans, tomatoes, celery, and asparagus. Thus, two groups of Chinese, speaking different dialects and specializing in different crops, lived side by side in fragile symbiosis. The destruction of their homes by fire in 1915 ignited their cultural antagonism, which worked in tandem with the dictates of geography and agronomy to precipitate the founding of Locke.

In 1907, the Sacramento Southern Railroad, a subsidiary of the Southern Pacific Railroad, had built a line from Sacramento to Walnut Grove to facilitate the export of asparagus from the area. The Southern Pacific established a packing shed on the wharf just north of Walnut Grove in 1909, which attracted Chinese workers. To cater to these workers, Chan Tin San, a Zhongshan merchant, built a one-story store and saloon in 1914 on land leased from the heirs of George Locke, who had died in

1909. Locke had a business selling window shades, blinds, wallpaper, and carpets in Sacramento, and had invested in 490 acres in the area north of Walnut Grove, which he planted to Bartlett pears. Soon after Tin San (who was known among whites by his given name, Tin San, rather than his family name, Chan) opened his store, Wing Chong Owyang built a boarding house, while Yuen Lai Sing constructed a gambling house next to Tin San's building. These early businesses reflected the needs of a semi-migrant labor force, whose members needed rooms to sleep in, a store to shop in, and a gambling house to relax in. These buildings became the nucleus of Locke.

The leader of the Zhongshan merchants from Walnut Grove was Lee Bing, who along with six others provided the capital for the construction of a restaurant, boarding house, drygoods store, hardware store, two gambling halls, and a town hall which eventually housed a Chinese school. The actual construction of Locke was carried out by white carpenters.

For some five decades Locke was inhabited solely by Zhongshan Chinese. Although Chinese exclusion was in effect, the Delta managed to draw new immigrants—both male and female—well into the 1940s, as the oral histories in this book show, because agriculture in the area continued to provide a living to the Chinese in this relatively secluded section of California. The work was backbreaking, but one earned enough to survive. Perhaps just as important, one could scratch a subsistence from a small plot of ground by growing vegetables, melons, and other crops, and by fishing in the many sloughs. Almost everyone whose story is told in this book mentioned a love of fishing, which not only provided food but was a form of recreation. Besides, as Mrs. Jone Ho Leong recalled, one could purchase a large amount of pork entrails and other "undesirable" meat cheaply from the slaughter house for next to nothing. And during the Prohibition era, with whites descending on the town every weekend to drink, gamble, and cavort with prostitutes, residents of Locke made money serving these funseekers.

The Delta was one of the few places in rural California where Chinese families were established. Before Locke was founded, Chinese women had begun to settle in the Delta. The 1900 census counted fifty-nine married Chinese women in the region, twenty-one of whom were married to merchants, nine to other kinds of businessmen, two to laundrymen, five to professionals, six to farmers, ten to farm laborers, and six to cooks and common laborers. Wives were considerably younger than their husbands. As few Chinese women emigrated, and the majority of those who came in the nineteenth century were made to work as prostitutes, American-born Chinese nubile females were very much in demand.

Twenty-one of the fifty-nine wives of Delta Chinese residents in 1900 were born in California, one in Idaho, and the rest in China. Perhaps because their mothers were American-born, the children in some Delta Chinese families had American names. A number of them attended a missionary school, others enrolled in segregated public schools, while all of them went to Chinese school after the public school let out.

By 1910, there were only twenty-six resident Chinese wives in the Delta. Ten were married to merchants, seven to farmers, two to common laborers, and one each to a boardinghouse keeper, a cigar-stand owner, a clerk, a shoemaker, a winemaker, a farm foreman, and a farm laborer.

Though their children had to enroll in segregated schools, and the social hierarchy and racial division of labor were rigid—with old stock Americans and immigrants from Great Britain and Germany owning the best land, leasing tracts out to Chinese, Japanese, Portugese, and Italian tenants, who in turn hired newer and darker-skinned immigrants to work for them—Chinese in the Delta, especially those living in Locke, felt comfortable in the area. The deep attachment that Locke's inhabitants have to their village is best expressed by Bing Fai Chow, who said, "In the past, the whites would attack you with stones when you walked through some of these towns. We never dared to walk on the streets alone then—except in Locke. This was our place."

Our place, indeed! Locke is not just the last rural Chinese town in America; it has been, and will continue to be, a testament to the tenacity and courage of Chinese immigrants in California.

Sucheng Chan
Santa Cruz, California

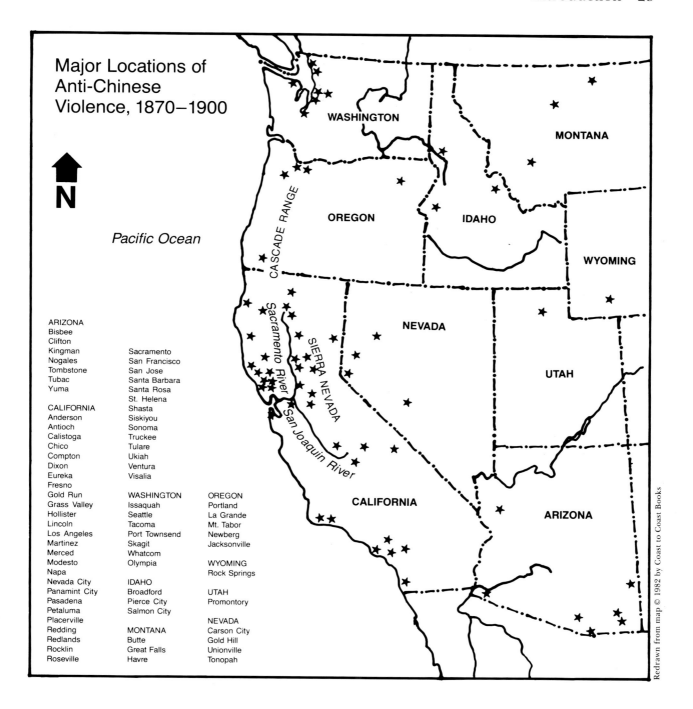

Major Locations of
Anti-Chinese
Violence, 1870–1900

N

Pacific Ocean

WASHINGTON

MONTANA

OREGON

IDAHO

WYOMING

NEVADA

UTAH

CALIFORNIA

ARIZONA

CASCADE RANGE

Sacramento River

SIERRA NEVADA

San Joaquin River

ARIZONA
Bisbee
Clifton
Kingman
Nogales
Tombstone
Tubac
Yuma

CALIFORNIA
Anderson
Antioch
Calistoga
Chico
Compton
Dixon
Eureka
Fresno
Gold Run
Grass Valley
Hollister
Lincoln
Los Angeles
Martinez
Merced
Modesto
Napa
Nevada City
Panamint City
Pasadena
Petaluma
Placerville
Redding
Redlands
Rocklin
Roseville

Sacramento
San Francisco
San Jose
Santa Barbara
Santa Rosa
St. Helena
Shasta
Siskiyou
Sonoma
Truckee
Tulare
Ukiah
Ventura
Visalia

WASHINGTON
Issaquah
Seattle
Tacoma
Port Townsend
Skagit
Whatcom
Olympia

IDAHO
Broadford
Pierce City
Salmon City

MONTANA
Butte
Great Falls
Havre

OREGON
Portland
La Grande
Mt. Tabor
Newberg
Jacksonville

WYOMING
Rock Springs

UTAH
Promontory

NEVADA
Carson City
Gold Hill
Unionville
Tonopah

Some Anti-Chinese Laws

1852　Foreign Miners Tax revived to apply to Chinese (California Legislature)

1854　Prohibition of Negroes and Indians from testifying in court either for or against whites made applicable to Chinese (California Supreme Court)

1860　"Mongolians, Indians, and Negroes" barred from California public schools (California Legislature)

1872　Chinese barred from owning real estate or securing business licenses (California Legislature)

1879　Chinese excluded from employment with corporations, and with state, county, municipal, or public works projects (California Constitution)

1882　Congress passes Chinese Exclusion Act, barring Chinese laborers from immigrating for ten years. Chinese officials, teachers, students, merchants, and travellers exempted. Naturalization forbidden to all Chinese.

1888　The Scott Act invalidates Chinese re-entry visas, stranding over 20,000 U.S. workers overseas

1892　Chinese Exclusion Act extended for ten years. Chinese laborers already in the United States required to carry certificates of residence.

1904　Chinese Exclusion Act extended indefinitely, and expanded to cover Hawaii and the Philippines

1906　Anti-miscegenation law extended to Chinese (California Legislature)

1913　Alien Land Act, prohibiting persons ineligible for citizenship from owning land (California Legislature). Similar laws were adopted in Arizona, Idaho, Oregon, Washington, and five other states. Declared unconstitutional in 1952.

1922　Immigration Act excluded "Chinese women, wives, and prostitutes" from coming to the United States. It also provided that any woman citizen who marries an alien ineligible for citizenship (e.g., Chinese) shall cease to be a citizen of the United States.

1943　Chinese Exclusion Act repealed, replaced by a quota on Chinese immigration of 105 per year. Many more Chinese enter annually as non-quota immigrants. Chinese allowed to naturalize.

1965　Immigration and Nationality Act raises quota of Chinese immigrants from 105 to 20,000 a year, on equal footing with other nations.

BITTER MELON

Inside America's Last Rural Chinese Town

Ping Lee

Born in Locke in 1917, son of the town's co-founder, "Charlie" Lee Bing, Ping Lee today is one of only a handful of first-generation Chinese still living in Locke. At the age of seven he was sent to live on his father's farm in Grass Valley, California, near the Sierra foothills, primarily to attend an integrated school rather than the segregated schools of the Delta. To ensure the quality of his son's education, Lee Bing donated the land the school was built on. Then, despite losing much of his holdings in the Depression, Lee Bing also helped finance his son's education at Sacramento Junior College, and a B.S. degree in Economics and Business Administration from the University of California, Berkeley, in 1941. Today Ping Lee is the unofficial Mayor of Locke, and proprietor of The Big Store supermarket in neighboring Walnut Grove. He is an open, friendly, and voluble spokesperson for Locke and its colorful history. He is also an avid San Francisco Giants baseball fan, traveling down to the city half a dozen times a year for games. Here he recounts the story of his father's eventful life in America and his contributions to Locke.

Locke co-founder "Charlie" Lee Bing, with his wife Lee Bo-ying, and sons On, left, and Ping Lee, 1920. *The Chinese "Godfather" of the Delta, Lee Bing used his knowledge of English and friendship with powerful Delta landowner Alex Brown to rise from field laborer to wealthy entrepreneur by the turn of the century. For the next fifty years Lee Bing operated two gambling halls in Locke, a restaurant, hardware store, drygoods store, herb store, and a combination barbershop/pool hall, and served as Delta chairman of the Chinese Nationalist Party (KMT). He was one of the region's largest Chinese sharecroppers, a "boss" who recruited cheap labor for area ranchers for a share of their wages. (Photo courtesy of Ping Lee)*

WELL, WHAT DO YOU SEE when I sit here? You don't see a white man here. You only see Chinese. Yet I'm American born. So my thinking's all Chinese. That's all I remember about Locke—lots of Chinese. That's all there were. There wasn't any Caucasian people that came here. But I also learned occidental thinking. That was brought on by my father. My father was a strong believer—he believed this was the greatest country in the world.

I was born in Locke. October 1917. My father's history here, of course, is a long, long history. He came over in 1893, at the age of twenty-one. He's from Zhongshan, about a half hour north of Macao. He came over here with the Chicago Expo, the World Fair at Chicago. They wanted to get some of this background on the Chinese with their queues and their hats

. . . landed in San Francisco, took him to Chicago, stayed there a couple of days, that was the deal. Then he came back to San Francisco. He had "white papers" just like 75% of the people did in those days, before the turn of the century. You bought papers to come here, you know. When he come up here from China, he was nothing but a sheepherder. The Expo deal was, you came over here and you paid your $500 or $700 and you jumped ship. So he jumped ship, and here he was. Lots of them did that.

During that time the harvest season came up over here, just across the bridge, and he started picking pears and all that. [Walnut Grove's] Chinatown was up here where the liquor store is, in that area. It was booming; it was the biggest Chinatown on the river. But anyway, he's working on the ranches and he decided he didn't want to work that way for the

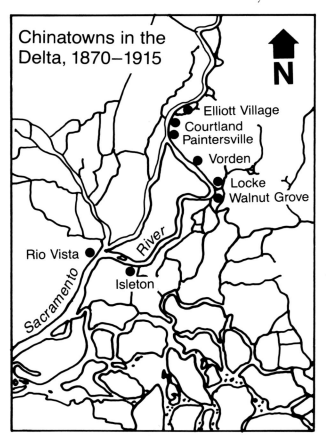

Chinatowns in the Delta, 1870–1915

N

Elliott Village
Courtland
Paintersville
Vorden
Locke
Walnut Grove
Rio Vista
Isleton
Sacramento River

rest of his life, coming over to the Gold Hills. He said that's no way to get ahead, so he came up here and made a lot of friends in town, and met an old cook here—name was Lee, old guy, maybe late fifties, sixty years old. He worked for Alex Brown. Alex Brown, of course, owned everything then in Walnut Grove. He'd been the kingpin at that time for about twenty years. His mother ran the Walnut Grove Hotel and the boardinghouse, and Alex was working for van Löben Sels. He had all this land—I don't know, van Löben Sels was associated with a bank or something. He got all this reclamation land, what you call it, all the way from Twin Cities Road all the way further, into south Sacramento around Parkway. All that land. Alex Brown was like a superintendent and he was watching things for van Löben Sels. So Alex Brown was a big man here. He hadn't started his bank yet, but he owned everything else.

Well, my father, naturally, just like any of the young Chinese when the nighttime comes, he come up to this booming town with gambling, maybe a thousand people, thirty or forty businesses, primarily Taishan people. But he's Zhongshan, and there's probably only ten or twelve Zhongshan merchants. Zhongshan, Taishan, all right, we're speaking of a district. Zhongshan is a half hour north of Macao. Taishan is further, over a mountain range. Now, in China, in the old days, you would never be on the other side. You wouldn't marry anybody on the other side. Stick on this side and speak a different dialect, that's the way it was . . . It's not so much when you say, just because you say I'm Zhongshan and you're Taishan that I hate you—I wouldn't put it in that kind of category. But you've got to remember that the two dialects are completely different. It's just like speaking English and Chinese . . .

Anyway, he meets this old cook, Lee, and asks him, "Can you get me in here? I'll help you, if you teach me how to cook." That's where he pick up the name Lee, you know. My family name is "Kan." Ping Kan Lee. Anyway, Lee tells him, "Serve your apprentice, you can't just cook," and my father says, "I'm willing to learn."

Finally, Alex Brown did hire him. Alex liked him. He progressed very fast. He learned how to write Chinese, and nighttimes he goes to a Caucasian woman, a housewife here in town, who teaches him how to read and write English. After a while he spoke as much English as most anybody on the river, being Chinese. He became a cook, a chef, and Alex Brown liked him so much he finally said, "Get out of this kitchen. You're too smart for the kitchen. Get uptown and get some of that action." He only worked there for a little over a year, year and a half. [Then] he went uptown and he got a business for himself.

Now, *this* is the history of my father. He got into gambling and everything else—he bought a share in a gambling house. To tell you the truth, it's not easy for Zhongshan to get into gambling. No way. It's all locked up, OK? Taishan. But the gambling house wasn't doing so good. Still, it took a lot of guts if you aren't even one of them. They might come in and mess you up. That happened all the time. Down in San Francisco, oh, lots of times. But my father's ace in the hole was Alex Brown. Alex Brown owned all the grounds. He was the kingpin. There was no deal between him and Alex Brown, they were just friends. They admired each other very much. "Charlie" was a name Alex Brown gave him, though his actual name was Lee Bing. But he always called him Charlie. Or "Son." "Hey, Son, come here." But most he call him Charlie. A lot of the old guys today still call him Charlie Bing.

My father didn't care. He played it to the hilt. He walked the streets because Alex Brown was the kingpin. If he had any problems he just went to Alex Brown and it's taken care of. He was a white man, he owned everything. He was a big man. Alex Brown just put the word out: "You touch my boy, everybody loses . . . everything locks up."

In seven years, my father's got seven businesses in town. The man is very brilliant, the

Identification Cards: Lee Bing and Lee Bo-ying. *Chinese, unable to become U.S. citizens until repeal of the Chinese Exclusion Act in 1943, were required to carry identification cards like these at all times.*

history already shows how brilliant he was. First off, he became an herbist. Where he learned it, I don't know. Herb store maybe. Then, there are two gambling houses. A restaurant. A hardware store. A drygoods store, and the other one he ran as a barber shop and a pool hall. On this side, down Market Street where the Porthole is—that's where he had a gambling house. In those days it was up on stilts. You've got to remember everything was like the wharves in San Francisco, because it floods. So the street itself, there's no bottom street. You can walk underneath it, but you have to duck a little bit, that's what Han Lee tells me.

So anyway, from there he started making a fortune. In seven years he becomes very prosperous, he goes home to China to get married. He was also very, very patriotic. At that time—you're talking about turn-of-the-century now—Dr. Sun [Yat-Sen] was already beginning the revolution in China. He's attempted many times and been defeated. Ten times before he was going to overthrow the government, but at that time, everything began to roll.

In the meantime, my father has worked underground here because he was a rich man, so he gave a lot of money to the cause. Then he goes home to China to get married. It's about 1904. He went back there, toured China, he got married, built a house. That was typical when you become prosperous. You to back to your village, you build a house. He also had a father there. He was an old man. He went to Australia when they found gold over there, but my father said he went a poor man, and he came home even poorer. That's possible. He said it was. He said he found nothing.

So my father built a house and my mother, married, comes to the village to live in the new house. They probably met through matchmaking. See, my mother's family was rich. They were all scholars—her great-grandfather was a tutor to the emperor of China. We still have a piece of jade the emperor gave him, I guess it's priceless by now. You've got to remember now, my father was approximately 28 years old, he was already a rich man, OK? Who wouldn't want to marry a 28-year-old with all that wealth in America? They'd heard he'd made it in seven years; he was accepted as that young man that made everything over in America . . . My grandfather, naturally, my mother has to take care of him. He wasn't that old; about 60 I guess. But in those days, 60 is like 80 now. So my mother, being the daughter-in-law, has to take care of the father-in-law until his death. My father came back over after a year. My grandfather died in 1912, and my mother came over in 1914.

[In 1914, Walnut Grove's Chinatown burned to the ground for the second time in its history. All seven of Charlie Lee Bing's businesses were wiped out.]

He lost everything in the fire, all his buildings. They went into the gambling houses, took buckets. He told his nephew to grab all that money, don't take anything else, took it out of the safe. He had four buckets full of coins and some paper money sacked in there—somewhere between $6,000 and $8,000 in cash. His nephew took it all up there, back of the first hill, 8th Street, around there. Then he wanted to go back to the gambling house and get something else, so he tells the deputy sheriff, "You watch this money, OK, I want to go back and get something else." The fire was going, really burning now. The deputy sheriff says, "fine." But when he comes back, the deputy sheriff says he had to go down and get something himself, and when he got back, all the money was gone. He took it all. And you know, within eighteen months, that guy died. Cancer. He suffered like hell. All the Chinese say, the money he steal, that's what happened. My father, he didn't even have enough money to go back to China after that.

So when the town burnt down, my father went up—this is the true history. This is the biggest thing I've spoken to the historical society about. You got to have a reason to start. After this burned up, why not rebuild in Walnut Grove? Why did my father select Locke? For the simple reason Tin San Chan and Wing Chong Owyang are two Zhongshan people. Wing Chong was a carpenter and a laborer. Tin San Chan was a big man, a real fireball. He was about ten years older than my father. He would have been the biggest man on the river but unfortunately he gambled a little bit and all that, and he never made it big. He made it, and he lost it. He spoke very good English for a Chinese, so he supplied the Chinese labor.

So when Walnut Grove burned down, the idea was, you got to start all over. But you can't buy land. Chinese can't buy land in those days, you've got to remember that. [Under terms of the 1913 Alien Act, aliens ineligible for citizenship could not own land in California; the Chinese Exclusion Act disqualified all Chinese from naturalization between 1882 and 1943.] You've got to rent it from somebody. That's why I say the man had such foresight. He said

"why not go up to this ranch where its all full of pear trees, with these two buildings sitting on the edge of the ranch serving the people?" One was a lodge, with Yuen's family there, and the other one was sort of a beer joint. The wharf was already there, part of it, not quite extended, the middle part. And they were shipping asparagus and celery out in those days. Chinese worked on it. They shipped it out—there was no such thing as a motor truck or a train up here then.

And because they were all Zhongshan, they got the idea, why not build the town here instead of going back there? With that idea, the eight or ten Zhongshan merchants [from Wal-

Alleyway, ca. 1925. Scenes like this were characteristic of the Delta's Chinatowns. Its gambling houses, whorehouses, restaurants, speakeasies, theaters, and markets attracted as many as fifteen hundred people to Locke on weekend nights during the 1920s and 1930s. It was a wide open town with no laws, no sheriff—and therefore no recorded crime. (California State Library)

nut Grove] had a delegation—my father was one of them. They went up to see George Locke [an heir of the original George Locke, who died in 1909], and talked about it. No problem. You can always build back to the levee this way . . . then continue on this way and build a town. Then they shook hands about how much rent. This is all history now, exactly what they did. They never changed their mind. It's how the town was built, in 1914.

All that thing [Locke] was finished inside of a year. The main street and the backstreet where I live, and where Mr. Jang's museum is, all that area, was built then. Some of the carpenters came in from San Francisco, some from Sacramento probably. It's the only American town built by Chinese. Not Chinese labor—Chinese capital. Two of the workers I knew very well. One was Cleveland Hill. You won't know him, the one who started the house of ill repute, and had the bar next door to where I live now. He was a good friend of my father's. He came up here to build the gambling house and build my father's store. He loved to gamble. My father had the gambling house going already. As soon as the town was being built he had it going. Every Saturday, Cleve Hill, about twenty-one years old then, six foot two, big guy, drunk all the time, he'd go in there and gamble at my father's place. Blackjack. Fan Tan. He told me this himself. When I came down here he helped me build some of the stuff and he was an old man then.

He told me, "Your father was a good friend. I never forgot that guy." He said when he was running around wild, he'd come up here and get his paycheck and start gambling and fighting; and Jesus, you know, my father, he says, he took him aside. He said he wants to talk. "You better stop gambling." He says, "You're a pretty good carpenter"—I guess he was an ambitious guy—he says, "You like to stay in this area, but you better not gamble. My door is open and I welcome you. I know I can take your money eventually, but being a friend,

take my advice: don't gamble. You can't beat it, you can't beat the house."

Anybody tell you that, Cleve says, has to be good.

I said, well, I know my father told all his friends not to gamble. But I don't know why he started a gambling house. He got so many things going. He's got four or five ranches, and shared some other property, sharecropping.

OK, the way labor sharecropping worked in the Delta—let's say you're the [white] landowner. I'm the Chinese guy, you don't care what it is—you know me, you trust me. I say, hey, let me run this cherry orchard for you. I am the one that brings the labor. I got to prune the trees, I got to harvest the crop, I got to put your field back in shape for next year. My father never works on them himself, but he brings in his boys. All you do in those days—it wasn't that much when my father was sharecropping. He didn't have to pay for this fertilizer, airplane spraying, and all that stuff. Today the sharecroppers pay for it, but then you only paid for the labor. And it was split fifty-fifty when the pears are harvested, when the bills come in. You're not interested in how much I pay for labor. That's my business. I'm supposed to take that crop in and get that thing off to the market. All you furnish me is my ranch and my trees—and you better keep them up, and good. That's sharecropping.

So, he's involved in all that kind of stuff. In those days, sometimes you do make a few bucks. A share of this, a share of this . . . he's got four or five ranches, he's got his names out on [labor] contracts. In those days you hardly have to sign anything, you shake hands. "We'll do it for you"—and that was it. And if you're a white landlord and you got any problems, these boys aren't doing a job that you like, you come running to me. And my father'll go say, "Hey, what's going on here?" He straightens it out. That's part of his job . . .

That law [about Chinese not owning land] was pretty flexible. He bought a lot of land. He had businesses in Sacramento, Susanville, Weed, Shasta City, Oregon, Klamath Falls. But the most profitable of all my father's businesses were the gambling houses. He always said, "This is the business. I hate it. You can't count on it, it's illegal, the laws can change, they can lock you up." Though in those days they never arrested anybody. If you are arrested, by the time you get up to court, then you are bailed out already, you got your fifty bucks and you open again. They know it's there. Besides, my father had the biggest criminal lawyer ever bred; he was a city attorney, well known in Sacramento before he became his personal lawyer. They were old pals. Everybody knows Luke Howe, ask any old-time attorneys. Bald-headed, thick color, thick nose, everyday big car, had a chauffeur drive him to see my dad. I can remember the whole town come down here to Joe Chow's place, and my father had a beautiful store then. Luke Howe would be on the street then with all these Chinese people; if they don't know who he is, they'd say, "Who's that guy down there, Palm Beach white coat with a rose on it?" Oh, that's Charlie Bing's attorney mouthpiece . . .

In those days it's a necessity for the Chinese people to have a place to hang out. When you talk to anybody, they'll tell you that place [the gambling hall] served as a labor hall, a social hall. There's a lot of people I know went into the gambling houses and never even gambled. They went there and drank tea that was free, there's a pot of tea back there. There's musical instruments they play around with. Wong Buck, I don't know how long he has played those things. He likes Chinese music, you heard it. I can remember him. Wong Buck is about eighty years old now . . .

All right, they get back there [the back of the gambling hall] and we're all shooting the breeze, all the Chinese guys. Sometimes we play some cards—not gambling on the table, we just play among ourselves. We have no newspaper here. We don't even have a post box.

We're working the farm, now you've rented a room and you share it for five dollars—pay two and a half [a month]. When there's no work, you come uptown. You don't sit in your room, you go down to the gambling house because everybody's there. So we shoot the breeze and you happen to come back from China, maybe I've sent a few bars of soap you took to my family back there, telling them I'm all right, maybe next year I get a few bucks and I come back see the family myself.

So I see you, and you tell me the news. That's one way it serves. The next way is, nobody has any post box in town. Back of the gambling house there is a post slot where you can slip the papers in. You would come in town after a week on the ranch and look, you got a letter, you take it, it's yours. Or else, you didn't come up town but you work together and you see his mail and you take it back to him. Serves as a post office. Or a bunch of you might be horsing around playing pinochle back there, and somebody from Dennis Leary's ranch or Joe Blow's come up needing six guys to clean up and get ready for fruit picking . . . you go in there and see three of us sitting in there and you say, "Hey, you guys working?"

And we say, "No, we just finished a job last week."

"Hey, you want to go down to my ranch, do this, yeah? We need three more."

"Oh, we could find you three more."

"OK, in half an hour wait for us in front. Go get your blankets and stuff and we'll go down."

That's how they find you.

It was a crazy time. You're talking about a thousand Chinese working on these farms around here—the town was all Chinese. The Mexicans came in in the fifties. Mexicans never gambled in those places; Filipinos came in the thirties from the islands. They loved to gamble, and they played the Chinese way. The Filipinos and the Chinese. And the Japanese wanted to gamble. At one time Locke had four or five

Courtland's Chinatown, ca. 1910. Driven from the countryside throughout the West by anti-Chinese violence in the late nineteenth century, Chinese laborers took refuge in the backstreets of communities along the Sacramento River from Rio Vista to Marysville. Courtland's Chinatown, once the largest on the river, burned in 1930. When the owners refused to renew their leases, most Chinese moved to Locke and Walnut Grove. (La Vern Studio/Frank Cowsert)

[gambling halls]. The town was all business, going until about 10. There was some trouble, but never after 1930 or so. But in the early twenties, before 1924, you had tong wars—over gambling, somebody trying to muscle in . . . But there again, during one war my father said, "If I stay in town there'll be a lot of bloodshed." Rather than do that he locked up his place and left, went up to Stockton. He could have stayed here. But he said no, they're all people who worked for me one time, I'm not going to stay here and create bloodshed just because we don't belong to the same association [tong]. My father had a hatchet man protecting him all the time. He didn't build up his empire by being scared, you know. They even shot at him—and missed, that's all.

By the forties in Locke, there were only two gambling houses, [both] owned by my father. My father's gambling houses lasted the longest, longer than any other place on the river. He started about 1908 when he had gambling in Walnut Grove, and lasted until 1951, when they decide to clamp down. That's a lot of years. Nobody else lasted that long.

My father didn't even like gambling, but he had to manage the place. Most of the time he'd be talking politics in his headquarters in Joe Chow's place—political headquarters. He was [Kuomintang] Chairman of the district for a long, long time. District was called the Delta. They had lots of people; you can see their pictures in the museum when Dr. Sun [Yat-Sen] died and all that—see how many people there were. My father was a rich man, so he gave a lot of money to the cause. A lot of overseas [Chinese] gave a lot of money to Dr. Sun's revolution. Dr. Sun was a Zhongshan, you know. My father met him once in San Francisco, on the

The Young China Association 比美洲萬華中國同盟會 Courtland Cal. U.S.A.

street. It goes way back. My father was one of the originals. Way back. But my father never bragged about any of that stuff. He's a man who doesn't say too many things. He's not a publicity man. He believed in what you're going to do—let your deeds speak for themself.

I grew up in the Depression time. I didn't think I'd ever make it. The Depression hit my father, the same things as today, why some of these farmers are going bankrupt. He lost $80,000 on asparagus, which was a lot of money in those days. Like a million dollars. So he lost

Courtland, 1925. Gathering of the Delta chapter of the Kuomintang (KMT), to commemorate the death of Dr. Sun Yat-Sen, founder of the Chinese Republic. Courtland, like Locke, was populated by Zhongshan Chinese from Guangdong Province in southeastern China. Dr. Sun was also Zhongshanese, a source of considerable pride to many Chinese of the Delta. Tin San Chan, co-founder of Locke, is seated first row, seventh from the right. (Photo Courtesy of Bob Jang)

Ping Lee, star forward for the Locke Chinese basketball team, 1937. *Ping also played for Courtland High, whose student body was nearly one-third Asian from the 1920s into the 1950s. (Photo courtesy of Ping Lee)*

Ping Lee and brother, On, 1939, University of California, Berkeley. *(Photo courtesy of Ping Lee)*

that, and a thousand acres of land. His backer went bankrupt, a Miss Hughes, I remember the name. Big, fat, chunky lady, those days doing a man-sized job. She was shipping celery when the Depression hit, and went broke. She had to file for bankruptcy, and took my father down with her. But he never lost any sleep over it. He said, when you're in danger in anything, you've got to work hard to salvage it. But when there's no way you can salvage, don't waste your time thinking about it, brooding about it. Roll up your sleeves and go on to the next thing. That's his philosophy. And it's true. He says you can't, there's nothing you can do about it, why waste your time.

He was sixty-three or -four when I was the last year in high school, up in Courtland. And he tells me, "You have to go to college." I didn't have no preparation to go to college, and my father was broke. But sixty-five years old, and

he opens a restaurant in San Francisco so I could go to college. See, when I was young I lived in Grass Valley, where he had another farm, 120 acres. I went to school there. I didn't attend grammar school here, because the schools here were segregated, and he didn't believe I'd learn very much English and he believed that America was the place to be. He believed anybody born here should go off to college and learn all you can and get all this ability and bring all the knowledge back to China where you can open their minds, open factories, produce petroleum and all that. See, he was thinking patriotically. He was thinking of his country. All his life he was that way: be sure that you learn the things here, but also be sure that you keep the Chinese culture. No white man's got a culture like ours. So you keep the good things, you blend the two good things, and you have the very best of everything. In America you have all this technology, but they do not have our culture, they don't have the family, they don't have the integrity we have, they don't have the honesty we have. So you must preserve this. As a result, you grow up that way—you learn all of the Chinese philosophy of life.

Anyway, here my father's going to wait on tables so I can go to school. It was only 1941 by the time I came out of college—I graduated from Cal [University of California, Berkeley] with a degree in economics and business administration. But my father had a few bucks in his pocket by then. Things are pretty good at the gambling house, what he lost he forgot already. Everything's all right, would be for another ten years . . . my father often regretted that I wasn't born ten years earlier. Look at the empire he would've had! He wouldn't have to depend on all those cousins, right? I was twenty-some-odd years old. I was a young kid, but I also knew what the game was all about. I'm friendly with everybody. I know what's going on and I know how it's operated, what it takes to operate it. He wants to bring me back

Ping Lee in the butcher shop of his Walnut Grove grocery store, "The Big Store," 1975.

down here [from Sacramento, where Ping Lee ran a grocery store] to run his empire. But my mother didn't want me to. She didn't like gambling. Neither did he, but he's got to manage the place. So he wanted me down here. But then in '51 they shut down the gambling all over California. Big state attorney comes in—maybe his palms weren't greased enough . . . It was Pat Brown [former Governor Edmund G. Brown], before he became governor. That was one of his things. I understand his father was killed by a gangster, wasn't he? That's why.

My father died in 1970. Ninety-seven years

old, died of old age. But right up to the end he could still give you advice. That's one thing I always treasured, the man was just absolutely fabulous. I say this not just because he's my father. His philosophy is terrific, his foresight: be honest, think big, be a leader, not a follower, respect and always help those that are not as fortunate as you, never do anything that dishonors your family. At six years old he pushed me on the stage to speak on a national holiday. I'd cry, I couldn't remember what I was supposed to say. I was brought up very small to speak in public, when my father would have all those parties. In a way, it's probably that I had the early training and I did have education later . . .

I have a wonderful life. I can't compare myself with these old people [in Locke]. You know I love them all. Just go down the street and ask them . . . As far as the old people is, I *should* do better than them. I have the education. They don't know the American language. I do. I went through college. I ran a store for forty some odd years. I worked hard at it. It's not all in vain because I'm very happy. Like my father said, the trees are all cut down now, you can see the light. You can walk easier. That's true. I didn't have it quite as hard as my father. My father did open the forest for me. He may not be too successful chopping the trees down, but I chopped them all down. He had to show me where they all were first. He didn't chop them down but I did. So that's all right.

There are hundreds of Chinese merchants in businesses like mine, I'm sure. I could probably say that I've been very successful at it—I worked very hard at it. First thing comes is pride. Got to have pride in what you are doing. And hard work never killed anybody. It's the worry that kills you. And I work very hard at it. I was brought up that way. My children are brought up that way. Chinese always have.

Wong Yow, with winter melons from his garden, 1975.

Wong Yow

As a long-time orchard worker, gardener, and handyman for the Leary ranch outside Walnut Grove, Wong Yow was a favorite of the Leary children, who called him "King Yet" and relied on him for favors their own father wouldn't take time for—like fixing their bicycles. He was born Buck-Sing Wong in China in 1900 in the village of Yuan Feng, near Sheqi, the district seat of Zhongshan. His father emigrated to North America in search of work, and his mother died when he was nine, so Buck-Sing was raised by aunts. When he was twenty-one, his father paid $1,625 to an American merchant also named Mr. Wong to sponsor his son's admission to the United States as a "Paper Son." In 1921 Buck-Sing arrived for questioning at Angel Island about his "father," and passed admission. (The 1906 San Francisco earthquake had destroyed many records, and along with it the ability to trace legitimate heirs of Chinese immigrants. Laborers—and sons of laborers—forbidden to immigrate by the Chinese Exclusion Act circumvented the law by becoming Paper Sons to "fathers" like the second Mr. Wong). Now officially Wong Yow, he joined his father in the Delta, working a variety of farm labor jobs and living in the labor camps. In the off-season, he and his father shared a five-dollar-a-month boardinghouse room in Locke. His father returned to China in 1924. Between 1921 and 1935, working ten to twelve hours for a salary of a dollar a day, Wong Yow was able to save enough money to return to China in 1935 to get married, and purchase seven acres of rice fields. He returned to China again in 1947 and bought another eleven acres of farmland. After the 1949 revolution in China, he lost most of his investments there—and all hope of either paying for his wife and children to come to California, or retiring in China himself. Forced to continue working as a farm laborer (wages by the end of World War II had risen to approximately $1,500 a year; by the mid-1950s to $3,500), he continued to support his wife and son in Hong Kong. In 1968 Wong Yow was able to retire, and sent for his wife and two children to join him in Locke—33 years after their marriage. But unable to live on just his savings, Wong's wife went to work in nearby Delta canneries during the harvest season. In 1978, after becoming deaf, she was killed by a garbage truck backing up to her house.

ICAME TO THE GOLDEN MOUNTAIN in 1921, when I was twenty-one years old. My father had been here for about fifteen years before. He'd worked in Mexico first, doing fieldwork, then found out that wages were higher in the U.S. and came over here . . . My grandfather didn't want my father to come; he felt the work here was too hard, that he'd be better off in China. That happened with my *great*-great-grandfather too. He told my great-grandfather not to come over. You see, even my great-great-grandfather had been to Golden Mountain before. So there's this series of events, where my ancestors warned their sons not to come over here . . .

But it was my father who bought my papers for me to come over. It was my father who told me work would be available here. Actually, no one needed to tell you. It was general knowledge that work here was better, and you got better pay, and more work. Nobody needed to tell you that.

I came here by myself, on a ship. I didn't have a thing with me except the clothes on my back. You weren't allowed to bring many valuables in, or any valuables at all. I had my own clothes and a few pieces of luggage, and very little money with me . . . The trip took about a month or so, Hong Kong to San Francisco. I can still remember how crowded the ship was. We slept in bunkbeds in one large room, everyone kind of sleeping together. There were very few women on board. Those that were they kept separated from the men. They ate at different times, in different rooms. They slept in different rooms. We hardly ever got to see the women on board.

I was held on Angel Island for about two months, waiting for my witness to appear, being examined by doctors [and] answering dozens of questions. When my papers were approved, I went over to San Francisco for a couple of days, then came straight up here. My father was living in the Delta at the time. I had just finished learning to be a carpenter in

Wedding Day, 1935. *Wong Yow (top row, third from right) and his bride, Lai Yut Ng (directly in front of him), and family on their wedding day, Sheqi, China. Wong Yow was thirty-five, Lai Yut Ng sixteen. Wong's father (seated, center) had worked in Mexico and the United States before returning to China in 1924. Note western dress of men: it was highly prestigious then to return from the Golden Mountain with money and western manners. (Photo courtesy of Wong Yow)*

China, so I was ready to do that. Instead, I went straight to work in the orchards, picking pears and trimming trees. Tommy King's father was working in the same place when I started, over near Walnut Grove. There was plenty of work to do if you were interested in doing farmwork. We were making about twenty-five cents an hour then, and there was plenty of work if you wanted to do it.

I never did get to use my carpentry skills. It just wasn't done. Chinese people who came over to work usually went to work as cheap labor in the fields or orchards. They weren't expected—I guess allowed—to do anything else. Carpentry work was done mostly by Caucasians or some other culture. Besides, I didn't know how to speak English. That was my major setback right there. There were places that taught you English—there were schools open in Walnut Grove, for instance, that taught English—but because of my age, and because I really needed to just go ahead and work, I decided not to go to school. Actually, there wasn't any time to. Once you get here, you have to earn money to survive, and that's what I did. School didn't seem that important at the time.

I lived in Walnut Grove with my father for two or three years, then the fire burned down Chinatown there and I came to live in Locke. My father returned to China around then, in 1924. Many of the Chinese people who come to the United States don't like to stay for long.

Once they earn enough money, or believe they've earned enough money, they like to go back to China. Within a year or two of going back he remarried in China—my old mother, my real mother, had died already, so he went back to China to remarry. I stayed here and continued to work. Of course, I hoped to make a lot of money eventually. But the fact was, when Hoover was president we were making a dollar a day and work was scarce, so we had a pretty tough time. But as I say, I didn't really expect a lot. As long as there was a job and I could get some money coming in, that's what was important at the time.

I rented a room up in the boarding houses—the rooms on top, above Main Street there. Locke was a Chinese town; there were very few places suitable for us to live in like that. There were no Caucasians in town, the houses were all the property of local Chinese businessmen here. The restaurant called Al's right now, that used to be a Chinese restaurant. Then as years went by, it went through different hands and eventually Al got hold of it and turned it into an American restaurant.

The rent in the boarding houses was about five dollars a month, as I recall. There was a main kitchen, a common kitchen, but we each had our own bedroom so at night we wouldn't have to sleep together in one big room. There wasn't much to it—maybe half the size of this room here. There was a bed, one light. I had very few pictures on the walls or anything else. It was small, just enough for you to sleep in and maybe read the newspaper in, that was about it. We did have a window, but no sink for washing.

I hardly ever stayed there for any length of time, though. Most of the time we were out in the fields or the orchards, working. Most of us just rented a place [in town] where we could store our stuff when we left for work. We'd stay there when there wasn't any work to be done. But when you were working, you lived in the camps. You ate and slept right there in the camp most of the year. But every weekend the ranchers would provide a car and driver and send us back to Locke and let us stay for the day, usually on Sunday. We'd stay there the whole day, sometimes till nightfall when the contractor would come and take us back to camp. We could shop, walk around town, go to our rooms . . . Some of the men gambled. If you had some friends around you'd go and visit them. There were some families back on Key Street, but we rarely had anything to do with them. The children didn't want to play with a bunch of older men! It was a resting day for us on Sundays. Once in a while we would get together and go fishing: that was the main recreation at the time. There were times when we would go up to San Francisco, but this was very rare. There just wasn't time for pleasure trips.

A typical day in town might be to do some shopping, get my hair cut, maybe go to the movies. We would just sit on the benches on Main Street and visit, watching the people go by, or read the newspapers, it really didn't matter. It was just nice to have the day like that, the opportunity of going to town. For dinner I'd go to this boarding-type cafe: you had to be invited, but you also had to pay for the dinner. Or our employer would take us back to the ranch and we would have our dinner there.

I can't remember exactly how many people were living here. You mentioned 1,500 and that sounds about right. It was over a thousand people. Before, everywhere you looked there were people running in and out, and children everywhere. But those thousand people weren't actually residents of the town. A lot of them were from San Francisco. They'd come in on weekends, and even on weekdays, and go to the gambling houses or just hang around town. Gosh, I can remember all the businesses that were going on—the gambling houses and everything. Of course, you know about the gambling houses, and the gamblers who came into town. It was really exciting! They never caused any problems here at all. The gambling houses were all up on Main Street, and it was up to you

Freight ship, Sacramento River. *"In those times when the big ranches finished picking pears, they'd be taken in crates down in front of the landing area and shipped down to San Francisco. I remember going to San Francisco, or the other big cities around here. It was real easy to do. There used to be a train right in back, and it would take you to Sacramento or wherever you wanted to go in that direction. If you wanted to go to San Francisco you could pick up the freight ship. It stopped right in front of the Bank of Alex Brown there. You could just sail off to San Francisco, and it would bring you back too . . . It was very convenient in those days. More convenient than it is now. Today, there's not even a bus."—Wong Yow (La Vern Studio/Frank Cowsert)*

Farmworkers' barracks near Walnut Grove, 1973.

whether you wanted to hang around those people or not. If you didn't like gambling, you just stayed away, like I did. I never gambled. I never even worked in the gambling houses. There was always traffic going back and forth, and of course we would have to go up there once in a while to get our rides to work; but there weren't any problems at all. They didn't bother you, and you didn't bother them.

Life was busier in the camps of course, because we were working. When you weren't doing orchard work or picking asparagus, you were up picking grapes in Lodi. We got up at six and started working, and we worked every day for a ten-hour shift. For a day's work, you'd get a dollar fifty . . . They divided us up into different jobs. Some of us might be picking pears, some of us irrigating or doing other things. You just went to the job you were assigned to—every boss was different for each camp. But we were never mixed together, like Chinese and Mexican, or Chinese and Filipino. That never happened. We were always separated from each other. There might be other cultures at the camp, like Mexicans, but when it came down to working, we would be divided into Chinese groups, Mexican groups . . . we ate together though, in groups of eight. Our meals were included with our salaries, and prepared for us by cooks in the camp. The food varied with each camp—sometimes it was good, sometimes it was bad, there was no constant thing. At least we didn't have to cook for ourselves.

There was one big house for all the workers, and not everybody had their own room. There was one big room, and everybody had a board bed—a bed made out of boards, there weren't any cushions or anything like that—and the beds would be lined up side by side so everyone would sleep together in the room. I remember going to pick grapes in Lodi, they didn't even have a house for you to sleep in, or a bed. They kept us in stables where the animals were kept. We slept on the hay, or wherever we could find that was comfortable. Another example was after the pear season, we would go pick honeysuckle flowers [used to make herbal tea] in Sacramento. And when we went there we would have to find a place on the ground, that's where your bed was.

We got along all right with the Caucasians. I don't think there's any problems now. Now if you're talking about back then, maybe thirty, forty years ago, then there were some problems. They even had to separate the races—segregation, you know. But the Chinese workers didn't really associate with the American workers in the Delta, so there was no direct conflict in most cases. There was very little communication between the groups . . . when you're out there working in the fields, you weren't together, so what's the use of causing trouble? We were never put together with the Americans anyway, so this created some distance between us . . . It was mostly Chinese, some Mexican people. The Americans never really worked in the fields.

In 1935 I went to China, to Zhongshan, to get married. I remember when I got there they were celebrating [Chinese] New Year's. It was my family who actually knew the girl—knew my wife—and introduced me to her. So the courtship was started by them, but there still had to be some kind of consent between the two of us. It was still up to us whether we wanted to get married or not . . . Well, we got married that year, but my wife didn't come back with me right afterwards. She stayed in China. She didn't actually come to the United States until 1969, with my two children, a son and a daughter. They couldn't come until then mainly because it was so hard to get the immigration procedures through. They didn't allow you to bring your wife and children for a long time . . . my son was already twelve years old by the time he came here. After they all got settled down (I bought this house then, about eleven years ago), they came to work with me, doing farmwork.

But you know, I really enjoyed living here. There was always work to do, so I was pretty much satisfied. Picking fruit, pruning, irrigation work in the fields . . . there was plenty of work, and Chinese people I could talk to. I'll say the town has changed since then—now there's nobody around. I wish there were more people living in the town. But now there's nothing. There used to be buses and trains and ships going in and out of the area, people getting on and off. It was so busy back then, I do kind of wish it was like that again.

But I'd still rather live here in the United States than go back to China. I still have property there. I have a house in Zhongshan, but most of the land has been taken. Besides, the climate's better here in Locke. The air is good and clean. You get a cooling period in the day, but over there [Pearl River Region] it's hot all day long. Even at night it's hot. Wintertimes it does get cold here; we didn't have this kind of weather in China. But we got used to it. We'd work for a while and if it got cold then we would go where someone had built a bonfire, and there would be a huge pot of tea; we'd drink some tea and warm our hands and then go back to work. Besides, here you could earn more money. In China you wouldn't be able to raise enough money for your family.

Now I've got my own roots here—I've got my garden, and my friends here. I don't think I'd ever go back and live. I have family back there too. My younger brother is still back in China, with his family and his children . . . But my own children are here. My son, Kai, in fact, just graduated from Chico [State College] last month. I was very proud of him because of that. He graduated from the School of Communications. Did you know that both men and women

Family Portrait, 1976. Wong Yow, Lai Yut Ng (left), their son Kai (standing, right), daughter Ling Cheng (center), her husband and children, Key Street, Locke. Married in 1935, Lai Yut Ng could not join her husband in the United States until 1969, under terms of the 1922 Immigration Act. Although the law was modified in 1930, it enabled an average of only sixty Chinese women a year to enter the United States legally between 1931 and 1940. The purpose of such discrimination was to discourage the raising of Chinese families in America.

are in that same field? My daughter-in-law, Kai's wife, is also in communications—and they're both working in the same printing shop in Sacramento! My daughter is living in Vancouver, Canada, right now. She didn't like school that much; she never chose to go to college. She got married and now she's raising her kids, taking care of the family. She went through high school, and that's as far as she got.

I'd like my children to stay here [in the United States]. I wouldn't want them to go back to China, but I just leave it up to them. That's the way I've always thought—whatever they were happy with, I was happy with too. The best thing to do is to just let your children pursue whatever they enjoy. If you tell them to do something, and force them to do something, they're not going to do it. I saved money to support them through school if they chose to do that, but they didn't have to. Now they can do whatever they want, and if they want to go back [to China], then that's their choice.

No, I wouldn't want to live with them. If I was living with them, I wouldn't have the freedom I do now. I just do as I please, go as I please. It's very convenient this way. I'm not lonely here at all. I usually get up in the morning and make some breakfast for myself. And

Wong Yow in his living room, 1976. *"I like Locke. I like living here. The cities are never this comfortable." Wong Yow lives alone in his house on Key Street. He is studying to be a Jehovah's Witness.*

then I'll go out to the garden—at this time of year very early in the morning, while it's still cool. I work in the garden for a couple of hours before lunch, then I come in and fix myself lunch. Then, I'll usually stay in during the early part of the afternoon, just to relax, maybe watch some TV or read a newspaper. Then I'll go back into the garden around three-thirty, four o'clock, wnen it's cooled down a little bit. I'll go out to the garden for a little bit before coming back in to make dinner. Then after dinner I'll relax again and watch a little bit of TV before I go to bed! I can just come in and out as I choose, whenever I choose.

Translated from the Chinese by Connie Chan

Suen Hoon Sum

Eighty-seven years old at the time of our conversations, Suen Hoon Sum had clearly lost some steam. But his eyes were bright, his laughter quick, and with his deep, baritone voice he answered our queries with both passion and precision—with notable exceptions. Like many of his generation, he was skittish about discussing exactly how he got into this country, as if still fearful of deportation. Also, he was very reluctant to criticize whites, about whom he seemed ambivalent at best. Suen Sum is the first representative here of a larger social group historians call the Chinese "bachelor" society—men who came to the Golden Mountain to work, and who never married either by choice or because of legal and economic obstacles. With the equivalent of a high school education in China and the ability to read and write his language, the slim, gracious Suen Sum expected better from life than to be a farm hand. But he didn't speak English, and once in California as a Paper Son he became one of thousands of Chinese recruited by sharecropping "bosses" to work fields and canneries from Monterey to Alaska in the twenties and thirties. Between jobs he rented a room in one of Locke's boarding houses, while other Chinese retreated to San Francisco, or to "Second City"— Sacramento—in the off-season or when work was scarce. Long since retired from farmwork, today Suen Sum lives alone in his house on Key Street, in very poor health.

Suen Hoon Sum, in front of his home, 1976.

WELL, IT'S LIKE YOU EARN a couple of dollars in Hong Kong, but if you came over to the U.S. you would earn double the amount. It seems like everybody knew that. That's what I heard from my relatives who had come over here and gone back to China. That's what they told me. So I thought I'd come over and just try my luck. But thinking about it now, I would have been better off in Hong Kong. I probably had more opportunities in Hong Kong . . .

[To translator] I grew up in the same town as your mom, as your family did—Sheqi, in the countryside. I went to school. I had an education. I went to school at the age of seven, until about seventeen. I learned how to read and write Chinese. I did not learn how to write, or learn any English. If I did, that would have helped me, a lot. I just didn't have the opportunity at the time.

At seventeen I went to Omun [Macao] and worked at a bar for about eight months. After eight months my boss decided to send me to

Hong Kong to work. I worked in the Empire Theater—I think that's what it was called. I was working really long hours. I rarely had days when I slept more than a couple of hours, because I worked at night. At the time the Empire was about the second theater in that area, I think. I worked selling tickets. Sometimes I wrote the billing for whatever movie was showing that week. I didn't do farmwork or fieldwork when I was in China.

I arrived in the U.S. in 1924. I was twenty-eight years old. I was actually on my way to Canada before coming here. I didn't want to come here at first, but it was more difficult getting into Canada at the time, so I just wound up staying in the U.S. It was a Japanese ship, I remember—not very big. We took off from Hong Kong and most of the people on board were Filipinos. There were probably only about thirty Chinese in all . . . I was all by myself. I didn't have any friends with me. I had nothing with me except a few articles of clothing. I don't know, I guess those who came were usually those who were willing to work hard, and were dedicated. But by the time I arrived in the U.S. I was already too old, so it didn't seem appropriate for me to learn English . . .

You know, it seems to me there's no use in me telling you all this! I was just a simple worker, a farmworker around here. If you were to talk to a businessman or something, you'd probably get a better story than what I'm telling you. I don't see the reason for telling you all this. It's not going to interest anybody.

I was on Angel Island, like everybody else. There were a lot of people on the island at that time, a lot of Chinese—about seventy or eighty, I believe. I remember at meal times everybody just rushing at the food and trying to get what they could. When I left, I didn't come straight to the Delta. I think I got here around 1932. First I went to San Jose, and then to Santa Clara, I worked in the orchards there for a while. Once I got here there was plenty of work for me to do. It wasn't hard to find work if you

Asparagus packing house, ca. 1915. *The fine peat soil of the Delta enabled asparagus to grow very straight, facilitating packing and canning. Asparagus season lasted for about a hundred days, from March to June. Afterwards, workers moved from the Delta to California's fruit-growing regions. Labor bosses at this time also contracted workers for the Alaska salmon canneries. (La Vern Studio/Frank Cowsert)*

were just willing to learn how. There were lots of people staying in Locke at the time who didn't want the trouble of learning how, so they found it difficult sometimes. But there was work to do. I guess if you consider just making money for myself, I made quite a bit of money for myself . . .

Tell you stories about my working days? I worked all over the place! If someone asked me to work at a certain place, I went there. On the big ranches, around this time of year [July], I'd be working in the pear sheds and cherry sheds, or picking pears or whatever fruits they had in the orchards. I'd go to Newcastle, Auburn, pack plums and nectarines . . . then up to Lum Bun's and pack pears again. After packing pears in Walnut Grove and Locke, I'd go to San Jose . . . and after San Jose I'd come back to Locke and work in the tomato sheds, the tomato canneries until about November or so. Then I could either go to San Francisco for a week and spend some time there, or do whatever I wanted. It was very easy for a year to go by. Year after year you did the same thing—pick fruit and trim fruit trees. These are the two things. Every year it was the same . . .

I always had some kind of work to do, so I hardly spent any time in Locke for any period of time. I rented a room here and just left my belongings and went to work. You could rent a room for $2.50 a month here. There were a lot of people staying here at the time [the 1930s]. Three hundred or so residents. It was very lively, a very busy place. The businesses were in full run and Al's Place right now, it used to be a Chinese restaurant and people would be going in and out all weekend. There were always at least two gambling houses open, which kept the town pretty busy too, all kinds of people going in and out of town, mostly from San Francisco and people working the orchards. They rarely stayed for long periods of time, just like I did. The ones who came to work, they just left their belongings and went straight to the fields.

We even had a lot of college students come to the Delta to pack pears or cherries, that type of work. There was nothing else for them to do at the time. Canning work was the most available, so they would come flocking in to do it. It was real hard for the students. Very few kids even got to go to school then because of discrimination, segregation, those kinds of problems. We also had a lot of bad discrimination at work. There was an incident once in San Jose, where a farmer wouldn't let us work because we were Chinese. So we just came back to Locke. It's not like now, where there's equal opportunity and things like that . . .

But I got along with the Caucasians, I got along quite well. In fact, I joined a labor group with them—the CIO—when I was looking for work in the orchards. I was one of the very few Chinese who got to join up; and though the Caucasians knew I didn't speak English, they were still welcoming to me. Most of the tomato canneries had mostly Caucasian employees. I was one of the few Chinese working with them. There were CIO groups organized in many of the areas I worked in. The main ones, of course, were in San Francisco and Sacramento. In order to join up, you had to pay annual fees—no, seasonal fees, like five dollars for each season that you worked. For instance, if you worked for a couple of months in pears, you would have to pay five dollars for that. And another five dollars if you worked in tomato canneries.

When I was younger, fishing took a lot of my spare time. I would go out to the river with some friends, or go by myself and fish from morning to night. The fishing warden lived near me so even if I didn't have a license, he wouldn't say anything.

But I didn't have a whole lot of time for recreation. I worked almost all year long for just enough money to live on—about five hundred, six hundred dollars at the most, per year. I worked ten hours a day, and was paid from ten to twenty cents an hour . . . It's hard when you can't save any extra money. You work year after year, from youth to old age, and I still haven't saved any money.

Marriage? You can't get married without money. I never wanted to anyway. I didn't know how to speak English, so if I brought someone over here from China, she'd have to suffer like I did and work just as hard. I had some opportunities to get married but I just didn't want to; it would have put a double hardship on me and whoever I'd get married to. She wouldn't know

English and I wouldn't know English, and that's double the problems. Besides, I was always at work. I wouldn't be able to spend much time with her, or she'd have to go to work with me—with or without me, she'd have to go to work. So it would just be more of a nuisance. And if I married someone from here, from the United States who was born here, that creates a problem too. People born here and people born or even raised in China act different. People born in China have a custom, a tradition to go through. Most people born here don't care about Chinese culture and their own background.

But I never thought about returning to China either. After the Japanese invasion all my family was killed, so there was nothing for me to go back for. I never had the money to go back anyway. As for myself, I'd much rather live right here. I can go wherever I please and do whatever I please. If I were living in San Francisco I would have to spend a couple of hundred dollars a month for rent, and I'd have to worry about robberies and the people in the town. I'd be afraid I'd get mugged or something. Even if I had a few cents it would be gone—but I don't have to worry about anything like that here in Locke. Most of the people that live here are older men. Peace is what they are looking for, and that's what I'm looking for too. Year to year now I just sit and relax and walk around a bit, since I don't work anymore. I really enjoy the peacefulness and the quiet of the town.

I do wish there were more Chinese living in Locke, I really do. But that may never happen, and why should it? The younger kids grow up and they leave the town to find jobs. The older ones who may have gone to San Francisco want to stay there. So there's a constant decrease in the number of people living in the town. Most of them die here. Recently, two old people died. It'll be my turn soon.

Translated from the Chinese by Connie Chan

Picking pears, Walnut Grove, California, 1972. "The pickers and pruners were all Chinese until the early 1950s," says Suen Sum. Chinese were replaced in the fields first by Japanese, then Filipino laborers. The predominant labor force working the Delta today is Mexican.

Bing Fai Chow

The younger of two brothers born in China, Bing Fai Chow joined his older brother and an uncle in the Delta in 1921—and worked the next fifty years as a farm labor hand. Another of Locke's "bachelor" society, Bing was a fun-loving man who liked to drink and take off to San Francisco for a weekend of carousing. Until the 1970s his blue Mustang convertible was a local trademark, speeding locals up and down the Delta to their jobs or other pursuits. With a lifestyle that was low on frugality and high on live-for-today, Bing saved little money for his old age, so that now, in his 70s, he has fewer resources than his more pecunious neighbors. We interviewed Bing outside his room in a rundown boarding house in Walnut Grove. In visibly poor health, he had trouble articulating words, and his hands shook severely. Yet he seemed to enjoy the reminiscing, no matter how painful some of the memories.

COMING HERE WASN'T my choice. My family, especially my father, wanted me to come and help my brother out—to work and send money back to them in China. So it wasn't my own choosing. I wouldn't say I've been happy here, because I had to leave friends and family in China. But I wasn't unhappy. I don't regret it either.

It's just like in your own family [to interpreter], when your mother brought you here: you didn't know what you were going to do. It was your mother who told you what you had to do, just like my father told me. If your mother told you to go to school, you went to school. If she told you to go to work, you did that. It's a matter of what your own family wants you to do. At that time there were very few choices you could make for yourself. It's a fact of life that you either did what you were told, or you

wouldn't be part of the family . . .

Anyway, my home was in Zhongshan, in a village called Gong Medong, not far from where your family lived. My family had a farm there where we raised animals. Most of the people at that time, at least the wealthier ones, came over to set up businesses, but I came over mainly to do farmwork in the fields and orchards. I was about ten years old when I came over, in 1921. All I had was some clothes with me, and a few necessities. My older brother was already here. He was the one that sponsored me to come into the U.S. He's about ninety-three right now, and lives in Oakland.

I came here thinking I'd be able to go to school. But once I got here I never could, because of the discrimination. The schools were segregated—Chinese were separated from the Caucasians and so on. So I went directly to work with my brother, working out in the fields for about a dollar-fifty a day. It was hard, because I had to work right away and didn't have any friends. Two of my uncles had already

---

Bing Fai Chow in his boardinghouse room, Main Street, Locke, 1976.

Two Delta Chinese boys on their way to school, 1905. *The Delta's Asian children attended segregated schools until 1941, when the internment of the Japanese made separate schools economically unfeasible. Many Chinese were unable to continue their education in America, needing to work and make a living instead. Others felt too old to rejoin a classroom and struggle with a new language. (La Vern Studio/Frank Cowsert)*

come to the U.S., and I joined them afterwards to work in the fields. Then my second year here I began to do laundry. I was young then, so I could wash. The old people couldn't do it; they could only work maintaining white people's gardens, or picking weeds.

I didn't have any friends, and I kept thinking that life would have been easier in China. I did go to Chinese school for maybe half a year or so. But I had to leave as soon as my brother found more work for us. I just worked and sent my money back to my family in China . . . All I can remember was the hard work I put in. Chinese are always working. Other than that I can't remember too much. We worked right here in Locke, or out in the orchards. We lived in the orchards too. Working every day, or just about every day, you didn't have much time to play. There weren't many kids around anyway, living in the camps. When I did have some free time, or when it was off-season, I usually just swam or talked to the other folks. Swimming I guess was my main activity. There weren't any theaters around to go see movies, so we usually went fishing or swimming. I remember these American ladies who used to come around and try to get us to go to church and read the Bible and listen to their preachers. They used to offer us candy just to get us to go to church. We used to go to church just to get the candy, and then not stay for the whole sermon or the classes that they had afterwards . . .

I've been in Locke for about forty years now. Actually, when I first came here I didn't live in the town, but in a camp nearby set up in the orchards with the rest of the workers. Eventually I did rent a room here, and I remember the fire that happened in Walnut Grove. The Chinatowns in Walnut Grove burned down twice, you know. The second time was in 1931. I remember on that same day I was on my way to San Francisco and I couldn't get through because of the fire.

The first thing I remember about Locke was the gambling houses—there were so many gambling houses here. I didn't gamble myself. I didn't know how. But I had friends who gambled, and uncles who spent quite a bit of time in them. There were also a lot of children running around the streets. [To translator] I remember your aunt who lives in Walnut Grove right now who was the owner of Lim Kee's, and when her children were small they used to run around all over the place. I remember them distinctly.

The town's really changed a lot since then. I remember when thousands of people used to come through here on a weekend—three, four thousand people. Where there was farm work, you'd find the Chinese right there, and this was the place for farm work. There was no discrimination here either. Farther inland was worse. There were no Chinese and no Chinese newspapers there. Before the war, in Isleton, Rio Vista, places like that, the whites wouldn't take your order in the restaurant. You wouldn't even get served in the bakery shop. Chinese

Field barracks, Andrus Island, 1973.
Chinese field hands lived in barracks such as these for as long as ten months out of the year. Ranch owners provided them with three meals a day, which were deducted from their dollar-a-day wage. These barracks are currently occupied by Mexican farm laborers.

couldn't go to the bars. But now we can go anywhere. You can order anything you want to eat or drink and if they don't serve you, you can sue them. What happened was in 1942, 1943, a lot of Chinese served in the Army, and when they came back you couldn't discriminate against them. But in the past, the whites would attack you with stones when you walked through some of these towns. We never dared to walk on the streets alone then—except in Locke. This was our place.

I was one of the few people around here who had a car. I'd use my car to go to work in places like Castro Valley or Fresno, or even further than that, when there wasn't any work to do around here. It was pretty valuable to have a car then, be able to work in some other area than the Delta. Sometimes I'd drive to San Francisco with a couple of friends. In just one day you could spend a hundred dollars, and when you got back from the trip, you'd have to work again to get that hundred back. Working here was like fighting a losing battle. Just to earn fifty dollars you really had to work your tail off . . .

That's one reason I never got married, why I never had the desire to go back to China and get a wife, or find one here. I just didn't want the responsibility of having to take care of another person. When I first got here, I was working so much that there wasn't any time for anything like that. When I was younger I did sometimes want to go back to China. Even now I'd like to go back for a visit. But you need almost four thousand dollars now, and that's too expensive for me. If I had done it when I was younger and still able to work, I would've enjoyed it more. But back then I was just working and sending my money back to my family . . . now my mom and dad are dead, so there's really no reason for me to go back. There wouldn't be anything for me back there now.

I never got married, because I was pretty established here. I was free to go in and out as I pleased. But if I'd gotten married I would have had to worry about feeding another person and I wouldn't have had the freedom to just jump in my car and go . . .

I remember when I was about 27, 28 years old, I went up to Alaska to work in the fish canneries. It must have been 1938, the time of the World's Exposition at Treasure Island in San Francisco. There was a group of us went up to Alaska, a San Francisco labor group called the CIO [Alaskan Cannery Workers Union]. I worked up there for two years in the canneries. I liked the job all right, though eventually I got bored with it. But it was never a matter of liking or disliking your job. It was work, so you just did it.

What I remember best was how really friendly the Alaskans [Indians] were to us. We got along very well with them. I especially remember the girls there—they were very, *very* friendly. The Alaskans were a lot like the Chinese in many ways, though we couldn't understand what they were saying because they were speaking their own language. But when we'd go and catch deer or bear, the Alaskans would come along with us as our friends and help us. Some of the people there who were my friends said I wouldn't want to come back to the U.S., because we were picking Zi-kuo, a special type of fruit [berry] found only in Alaska—very good, sweet. But all I could remember was the incredible amount of snow that was there. You'd step outside and it covered you halfway up . . .

I remember it was about the 1960s, 1970s that I met your grandfather [to translator]. He used to go out in the orchards in Isleton where I lived and pick lemons off the tree and eat them just like that. I used to say to him, "How can you eat a lemon like that, isn't it sour?" And he said no, they're fine. After that I started bringing him oranges—and that's when we became friends. Once in a while he'd ask me to take him up to Sacramento to see a lawyer, and he'd tell me about a daughter in Hong Kong who's about fifty-four and I want to get her

family and her over to the United States. And guess who he was talking about? He was talking about your mom! I considered your grandfather as my very close friend. We were like family to each other.

Yes, it is kind of lonely here now. I'd really like to move back to Locke, but there's no room for me to rent there. I gave up my garden to your mom for her to take care of. I had to move out of the room I was renting because of the condition it was in. The roof is leaking and the doors are broken down. It's really hard to find a place now . . .

I wish there were more Chinese on the Delta today, but that's not going to happen. [To interpreter] Just take you, for instance, you and your brother. Now you're going to college, and as soon as you finish you'll be going out to the big cities and living there. Everyone goes to San Francisco to set up a business, or to do some other work besides farm work like their parents did. Also, many of the older ones who worked for a while have decided to return to

Boardinghouse kitchen, Main Street, Locke, 1975.

China. So there's a lot of traffic going out. Probably in another two years I won't be seeing you around here anymore. And your brother is sixteen, seventeen years old now? As soon as he hits nineteen or twenty, he'll be gone too, just like everyone else . . .

But I don't have a choice. I'm old now. I can't work. I have to live here. But I'd rather live around here, rather than in some place like San Francisco or Sacramento. The climate here is much better, and I can go anywhere I please without having any problems. Anyway, I can't forget this place. I've got all my memories here. About the only thing that can push me out of here will be a fire. I've already lived here for a long time.

Translated from the Chinese by Connie Chan

Effie Lai

We traveled to Los Angeles to interview Mrs. Lai, and found it worth every mile to meet this four-foot, ten-inch, husky-voiced, infectiously cheerful storehouse of Chinese-American experience. Unlike her equally dynamic—and diminutive—sister-in-law, Mrs. Jone Ho Leong, Effie Lai was born in San Francisco, a circumstance that gave her the advantage of English language and familiarity with American ways. In 1922 she married a prosperous Delta tenant farmer, who went broke two years before the Crash of '29 and struggled through the Great Depression as a dollar-a-day farm laborer. To help ends meet, Effie Lai worked as a pear sorter, tomato picker, asparagus canner, and bootlegger throughout the Depression, and later as a restaurateur, beautician, and translator for the California Department of Social Services. Her bilingualism gained her access to many circles in Locke; her stories are a veritable crossroads for many of the other Bitter Melon *subjects, including Charlie Lee Bing, Ping Lee, Ng So Yung, Jone Ho Leong, and Everett Leong. Today, Mrs. Lai lives in an apartment building she owns beside the Pasadena Freeway on the outskirts of L.A.'s Chinatown, along with her youngest son. She tries to rent her apartments to California's newest— and neediest—Asian immigrants: Vietnamese and Cambodians.*

I WAS BORN IN SAN FRANCISCO, May the 2nd, 1904. My folks came from a village in Zhongshan, on the Pearl River Delta, the village of Haotao. My father came over here before, in 1890, and went back the first part of 1900s and marry my mother. He belonged to a Christian church, and through the ministers back in Shanghai they got written letters substantiating that he was a Christian. My father was born in China, but he came on a citizenship paper. In those days they buy those papers; it's illegitimate in a way—illegal! I don't know how

he got a paper that says he was born in the U.S., but he wasn't. Or else he was saying he was the son of a native born . . . Anyway, when they came my mother was pregnant with me.

My father had a big family, a family of ten children. I was the eldest. He went to learn English at the Chinese Presbyterian Church, the one on Stockton Street. Those years he was poor. We lived in such a small quarter—a San Francisco flat. There were two bedrooms in back; back there is awfully dark so we slept there. And those days the conditions were very crowded, and there's lots of tuberculosis in Chinatown. My second brother under me developed tuberculosis and he died from that. He was only a year younger than I am.

Effie Lai in her living room, Los Angeles, 1986.

My father in the beginning was a garment boy. Then he has his own shop; when we lived on Clay Street my father rented a store there. The front, you see, is the factory, the back is where we live. And my father has about four workers, their job is to cut, design, and they doing suit garments, blouses, negligees for women. And my father had the long cutting table. We slept there too. Daytime was cutting table, nighttime was our bed. Three of us could sleep there, a cutting table is wide, you know. The front is the factory, and at the front there my father had a little candy shop. We were near to the Oriental School, so of course the schoolchildren at their recess come back and buy penny candies.

The men then were doing all the sewing. Now women does it. Then mostly men does, see, for men it's very hard to find a job, so they would put together some money and build a dress shop, and put in sewing machines there and they come and work from morning to six o'clock and do fine work. Not like the work they do now. Everything's silk at that time—blouses and negligees. Those were for the whites. Chinese don't wear those things. We all wear Chinese garments, good broadcloth cotton from England. My father even do circus garments, you know, the clowns, because I see the men was working there was sewing, stitching clown suits . . . and then one year when Chinese New Year come my father has a little money. He sent back to the old country and made me some beautiful garments, something like the Manchu Dynasty wears, that the queen, the empress, wears: big trimmmings and silk, silk dresses. Once a year we wear it for Chinese New Years. I used to go when I was a kid to church, to picnics to sing before big crowds—I don't know, when I was a youngster I wasn't afraid. I would stand there, big crowd at Santa Cruz when they had a big Christian convention, I would stand there with my Chinese headgear, beautiful dresses, and sing before five thousand people.

I went to segregated school, but it didn't interfere with me. The schools were segregated in San Francisco too, the Oriental school's segregated. I'm a good melting pot, you know. The children never say anything. I guess they get so used to it, they don't even notice it. That was the old Oriental school, right where the Chinese YMCA is now, and I finally graduated in the new Commodore Stockton school on Washington. I was the first graduating class. And then I went to Girls' High. I'm a dropout. I didn't finish school. In the evening I studied Chinese. I went to the Morning Bell Chinese School in Pagoda Alley [now Hung Ah St.], between Clay and Sacramento. That's near where we lived too, you know. Three hours, every day and Saturday also; three hours, six days a week. They teach you the classics, so we just memorize it and you don't know what it means anyway. I'm the only one in my family that succeeded and retained it. You see, I'm very Chinafied in a way, although I was born here. We spoke Chinese at home.

My father had set high ambition for me, that I should go to college. But those years he was poor. Where was he going to get the money to put me to school! So I married, that was in '22. I was married when I was seventeen years old. I thought that probably if I married I'd be free and do whatever I pleased—my father was awfully strict, you know. Wow. First thing is to get away from my family. Because at home I have to help to take care of the youngsters, help to do the washing, cooking—wow, that's a good chance to get away.

I married into Locke. My husband was a tenant farmer for the Meyer ranch. I met him through friends, and my uncle Wah Lee's merchandise store in Locke. I went up to Locke as a girl sometimes, to visit. It was so different from San Francisco's scenery. Coming from a big family, we lived in such close quarters. I liked to get away. And I love it, it's so nice up there. The weather there was nice, and the conditions—not the crowded conditions. Everything was so

spacious, to me, it was wonderful. . . Besides, when I go up there, I see Ping's [Ping Lee] mother—at that time she has no children—and then I stay with her. She has a house right on the river there. It's hardware store now. I remember that, beautiful place, neat and clean, beautiful accommodations, with so much airy space. Wow, it's the life for me . . . So every time when she asks me to come up, I'll come right away, I never hesitate. I get away from my home, and she treats me like a guest. I met her when I was in China. When I was about six years old, in 1911, when China was beginning the revolution, I went back to the old country with my uncle Wah Lee. My uncle went back there to get married. My uncle's wife is Ping's mother's cousin, Angie, see. So I met them first in Hong Kong. I've known them since I was a

Georgiana Slough, between Locke and Isleton, 1972. *The Sacramento–San Joaquin Delta is made up of more than seven hundred miles of such waterways, home to more than a hundred species of birds and an abundance of fish and wildlife.*

child. She comes from a very wealthy family in China; her brothers are all Ph.D.'s. Their family has money and educate the boys, and all her nephews and uncles are all Ph.D.'s and went up to Peking for the Civil Service Exam. I enjoy her very much, and I learned quite a bit from her. She likes me. I call her auntie.

At that time my husband, right after the First World War, they were doing pretty good. He was the head of the Meyer ranch there making four thousand a year—lots of money. There was two brothers there, Louis Meyer and Pete Meyer that owned big acreage on Grand Island, big acreage. It's orchards: pears, pea-ches, cherries. Well, the biggest crop is pears, that goes to the canneries. And they got a big beautiful home there. My husband, he got a Buick, what they call it? Those wagons, a big one, with side doors, you know, and you go open the side and there's a side wheel . . . it's a huge car, and expensive too. My husband likes the General Motors things mostly, so we have two or three Buicks. He's a pretty smart, intelligent man, although he's not educated, but he has that leader ability . . .

Anyway, when I got married it was the talk of the town. I marry in San Francisco, at the Fairmont Hotel. My father was very much

against it, because I was so young, and marrying a man older. My husband was twelve years older than I was, he was almost thirty. But they came to the wedding. It was a Christian wedding, our Chinese minister married me. We have a little banquet and when we came back on the ranch there, practically all the people from the river came. I guess they had around forty to fifty tables there, all borrowed from the different ranches because we don't have that much. At that time all the Chinese that work in the ranches, they're big cooks, you know. And they all come down and help, and then we have the best grub: shark's fin, all of those things, and then dried abalone, a real banquet. There were four or five hundred people there. I was married in January so it was a little cold, but it's nice as long as it doesn't rain.

I had my first child in September; I had five children altogether. Every weekend we'd come into Locke. Actually, if you could go twice a month you're doing good. That's the day . . . oh, that was the happiest day in our lives, the weekend, we go up to Locke. I'd see my uncle, Wah Lee, and his family. And all the people from the ranches come up here and congregate; catch up on the news—who died, who married, what's happening back in the old country, what's happening around the area there, the economic situation, all those things you talk about. And then during the summer

---

Wedding of Effie Jung and Lai Foong, January 19, 1922, in the Red Room of the Fairmont Hotel, San Francisco. Effie's father, George Jung, and mother, Chun See (partially hidden), are to her right. On the far right of the photograph is Effie's younger brother, Raymond Jung, who died later that year of tuberculosis. Lai Foong was the brother of Lai Fong, husband of Jone Ho Leong. Standing to his left is his Delta ranching partner, Mr. Zhang. (Photo courtesy of Effie Lai)

you see all the school boys from San Francisco come in and work on the ranches there, to pick pears. You see all kinds of mixtures, the ABCs and OBCs, you know. ABCs are American Born Chinese; OBCs—the overseas born. So we mixed together and the ABCs loved to come in because it's an outing for them. First thing, they earn a little money. Secondly, it's a vacation. It's so different from San Francisco, where you see nothing but cement and concrete. It's the open air, open space.

And Main Street, you couldn't get through sometimes, so many people. All the [Chinese] ranchers from the whole river congregated there. They sit around and chew the rags; there was a few ice cream parlors there, and pool halls . . . and the gambling halls, they flourish. The old hands, the OBCs, they come up and go in there and buy lottery . . . Then there's a whorehouse right next to Yuen Chong. That was a whorehouse when I first got married— two blondes in there. We called them white woman, you know, with golden hair. Big, husky, tall blonde. We'd see them, they'd dress up, walk down the street, we know what they are but they don't bother us. They sometime wear long gown, all makeup—in those days we don't make up at all, you know, we're primitive. So she's made up, she's pretty, you know that she's pretty, she's a blonde. And all the women would look like this [looks sideways, furtively] and then walk away. They all shy away from her. So conspicuous, you know. She stood out like a sore thumb. She doesn't bother us and we don't bother her. We Chinese always stuck to ourselves: she go on her business, and we go on to ours. The kids were always peeking, sometimes peeking into the window there. So we always said, "Don't you go in there!" We warned them, you know.

And there were Caucasians coming in. Those people come from Sacramento, San Francisco or Lodi, maybe Stockton, dressed up pretty good, they come over. At that time Stockton have gambling too, but not that's so open,

居樂
LOCKE, CAL.
國民學校
K.M.S.

美洲加省樂

Main Street, Locke, 1926. *The opening of the Locke Chinese School. (Sacramento River Delta Historical Society)*

---

see. Whites would come in to buy lottery—gambling, and the whorehouses. Even they said it's a dirty town, but you don't see a lot of the roughneck stuff. They patronize "Italian the Wop" [Al's restaurant on Main Street]. We always pass there, we know a lot of people, but we never even peek in there at all. We're not nosy at all.

Ah, there's lots of history! Sometimes I recall and sometimes I don't! Sometimes when you talk about it, then it comes back to me.

I stayed on the farm until, let me see, 1927—five years. Then I moved into town, lock, stock, and barrel. At that time we couldn't make a go of it. The Meyers lost it . . . the crop didn't bring any more money and they owed so

much, so they lost it [the ranch]. So when they lose it, we didn't have any money either because of the way sharecropping worked: the money is divided in half. So the owner gets half and we get half, but we don't even have money to pay for our groceries. They'd been losing money for two or three years . . . so we moved.

My husband went out and worked, and in those days it was terrible. A dollar a day as a ranch hand, and we couldn't get a job. So I went and worked, I lived with my children and went up and worked in the cannery there—Libby's. No transportation then, you can imagine from Locke walking up to Libby's, next to Clay Locke's ranch there. Every year toward the asparagus season there was hundreds of, I think they were Latinos, from in the East Bay there, from San Francisco, all come in to work there. Libby canneries, they have a bunch of shacks for the workers to live. The husband and wife generally comes in and then they have chil-

dren, some of them don't, they're all hands there; but we don't live there, we have to walk back and forth, so during dinner time, six o'clock, I have to walk home and cook for my little kids, and hurry up and go back there again. So it was really rough. Fifteen cents an hour!

And then when the season wasn't good, when there's no prices and the cannery wasn't canning that much, then experienced workers got the job; you got to know "who" before you get a job there . . . My husband at that time was working as a ranchhand, sometimes I don't see him for months. I'll be in Locke and he's down in Isleton, working day and night there, and he doesn't come home. If they're fortunate enough they come home weekly, but that's not to stay either: they come back and see you and go leave around four or five o'clock and go back with the boss, because there is no way of going home, they don't own cars at that time. Ah, it

was terrible in those days. We were so poor and with a bunch of kids, you don't even think of missing somebody. You don't think of those things.

[When I worked] I left my children home. My oldest son was only eight years old, he was awfully good. I taught him how to cook, he could cook rice on a kerosene stove. And then I said, now, when you get the dinners ready and the little ones at home, then don't go outside after dark. They're very good. Anyhow, sometimes they clean up the tables, sometimes don't. And my oldest son is only eight and he could clean up the little children and put them to bed. At that time no babysitter. So when I was working my mind is sometimes on my work, sometimes worrying about my children at home. But at that time, fortunately, times was peaceful. No kidnapping, no raping, no thing like that. You don't have to worry. We don't even close our door.

The worst was when the Depression came. My husband's out of a job. Couldn't get anything at that time; no social worker come down to the valley, and no way of getting anything. Sometimes you don't even have a dime in your pocketbook to get a loaf of bread. You sit at home, that's all. In those days our rent was only six dollars a month, and we're so poor sometimes we were only able to pay our rent. And the neighbors, when you were in hard time, you wouldn't even *dare* to ask the neighbors to loan you a dime. Because they're out there every day in that situation too. Everybody's in that same situation. But then fortunately, you have a few pounds of rice; and then what vegetables that friends from the ranch bring you down. You just eat vegetables, that's all. I don't fish at all. I'm not a fisherman; I don't go to the dirt and plant. We're from San Francisco, you know! I don't even get out of the door there. We'd just sit in the house. Then sometimes, it seems to me, the Lord takes care of me: some relations living on the ranch there, they'll bring down something to me but I wouldn't ask for it. Chinese are too—eh, what is it? Proud. Too proud. Sometimes you're stubborn for myself, but you have little children, you know, that you have to think of . . .

Wow, talk about bad times during the Depression. Sometimes I think back, you know, I was so fortunate I was so young at the time. [You] don't realize the situation that was so terrible. Today, no people exist like that. Nobody come down and help you, no welfare; to tell you the truth, all my life I raised my children, I never got a dime from welfare. I could raise my hand on that.

The longest I ever went without finding work? Oh, I think one year. I didn't have work at the cannery, that year the crop was poor, and during the winter I couldn't work because of my children. I couldn't go work in the tomatoes. And that year the season was short too, so that year was terrible. At that time, those Chinese were making bootleg, you know. And I didn't know how to make those things, so they taught me. They did it in the house there, on Key Street. My job was making the mash. When you make the mash, you got to buy the lowest kind of rice, the third grade, you don't use the good grade. And you've got to go up to Sacramento to buy it. And you put sugar in there, and Chinese ferment cakes—you have to go to San Francisco and buy those things. Small cakes, like a yeast. So finally, when they go and arrest those people, I got scared. Right next door, you know. There were only a few families that got caught. But I didn't hear about it until next day. They always come and raid them during the night. But you could smell it too. The odor permeates miles and miles away.

They'd sell it to the people who work, the ranch hands. They come down on their day off and buy it for seventy-five cents a bottle. I don't like it. In the mash, in the barrel, it smells good, but after it goes through that still there, it has no smell at all. But that taste there, I don't like that taste. But they like it. They say it's good—they call it rice wine. White in color. And they also teach me how to work the hydrometer too, to test the strength of it, so I could be a bootlegger too. But I got scared and stopped. Because in the first place, I don't believe in it either. But I'm trying to earn a little side money, you know. Everybody was bootlegging, making gin, Chinese gin, and selling to the people that has work. I got scared, you know. I said, "No, sir."

During the Depression things slowed down. And then the place seemed to be so dull; the Depression seemed to affect everybody. The gambling halls were open, but not as much gambler. They were operating on a deficit. And the people who worked in there, fortunately, they all have shares in there, so you don't have to pay them a weekly wages. If they do, they close up too. Fortunately, Ping's [Lee] father is the banker. So then if times is getting low, he could fork up a few until you're back up on your feet, and then you can plow it back again . . .

House on Key Street, 1975.

Sure, my husband gambled. Those days most of the Chinese gambled, that's the only pastime they have. I don't know too much about it, I'm ABC. I think he played lottery every now and then, and Pai Gow. They play on tables there, beads and things like that; and Fan Tan. But don't ask me that, I don't know those things at all. When he goes there I don't even know; he doesn't come home to tell you, because you know that it isn't right. But I know he does, because where else could he go? And in those days they have opium dens too, down in Walnut Grove. In those days, when I was first married, there were a lot of addicts. They don't stick the needles, but they go in the pipes, you know, in the bed there. They'd lay around, talk, that's the pastime. They didn't have theaters, no music. You know, Cantonese are not musical people at all. They don't go for music, they don't go for dancing. Nothing at all. In the first place, they're uneducated; they don't read much. So they have no way of entertaining themselves when they have time. So those are the people that came there, they're not educated. They're too busy making money to send back to the old country, they just don't have time to enjoy themselves . . .

My husband drinks too. One thing about Chinese though, they don't get drunk. They always drink at the family table, with our meals. But you know, my children now? My older son drinks; and my youngest drinks a little. My second doesn't drink any more. And then, they smoke; my husband was a chain smoker, until the last ten years when he had emphysema he cut out a little. Then afterwards he drink wine; when he couldn't take the hard liquor, he drank wine. He was a big wino. He died some twenty odd years ago. Wow, we went through a ride, rough there. It was awful. Fortunately, I think what pulled me through this, I was young. If this happened today, I die.

I had five children—three boys and two girls. We spoke Chinese, at home I jabber in Chinese. That's why all five of my children they understand Chinese and speak a little bit of it. Whereas the others completely lost it. But my children even now, even at my age now, when my children come home we speak Chinese.

They worked in the fields too. My first son went to work, right across Courtland, Sutter Island; the ranch is called Sunnyside Ranch. That is one of my husband's first cousin run that place for twenty years. So he went up there to work, picking fruit, doing odd jobs. The second son went up to Vorden, he worked there. Vacations only. We worked the seasonal, that's all. So my youngest, he was still young then, he went to the field to help his uncle, Everett's [Leong] father, to pick tomatoes— Everett's father and my husband were brothers, see. Wow, it's really hard work, back-bending, you know. So he was a youngster, he could do it real well, my younger one. He was about eight or nine years old. They paid by the box there. They don't pay by the hour. It's piece work there. They lose money if they pay you by the hour.

The rest of the time was school. You know where the road is to go to Lodi? That's a nice school there. And the principal, the last principal wasn't good at all. She's a woman, I've forgotten what her name is. She's very discriminating. Her nose is up in the air there. But she took care of the Oriental school too, you know. The white school was the Jean Harvie School there. The Jean Harvie School! Ha, ha, now we can bring back the kind of memories that we

Isleton, Main Street, ca. 1925. The fertile soil and abundant water supply of the Delta, coupled with cheap Chinese, Japanese, Filipino, and Hindu labor, helped establish the town of Isleton as "Asparagus Capital of the World." By 1910, Isleton was shipping almost 90 percent of the world's supply of asparagus from its docks on the Sacramento River. Continual planting with asparagus eventually exhausted the soil. Today the river region around Isleton is one of the largest Bartlett pear growing areas of the nation. In 1980, more than 120,000 tons of Bartlett pears were harvested here. (California State Library)

had. You know, after the segregation I didn't stay too long, because in '42 I'm down here already. You see, my last, Ervin, my third child, was the last one to graduate from that Oriental school. I went back for the graduation and since then we've never been back.

At that time Locke was a good place to raise children. All the children came out very successful, very nice children. Like my cousin's . . . all my uncle's children went to Cal . . . Main Street never bothered us. Those people never go in the back street at all. It seems strange, we got bars there, but no drunks. You don't see them. If they do get drunk in the bars there on Main Street, we're all in bed already in the back house, we don't see them. In that old house where we're living there, where my sister-in-law lived, I don't even lock my doors. I go up to Sacramento all day, I don't even lock my doors. Nobody come in and get anything. And even people next door, they watch over it for you too. And then we don't have strangers coming there. Believe it or not, I never encountered nobody that'll come in and harm us, and harm our children. Even the people who come in on weekends, they don't even come near our Second Street.

And then we have a whatchacallit, a man

that beats the gong—Bok Bok man! After twelve o'clock, every hour he comes along and beats the gong, and watch over things.

The biggest event that came in Locke was when General Tsai [General Tsai Ting-kai], the general, the Commander of the 19th Route Army [Republican Chinese Army] came and toured the United States [in 1934]. Wow, that

was a big event. I was one of the welcoming committee—have you see the picture? The long one? I was on the platform! The big, heavy-set woman is me. He was on tour because he was a hero; he fought the Japanese at Shang- hai in 1932. He came to visit us and he came to Locke, the main center of the celebration, and went up to Isleton and Walnut Grove, Court-

念紀影攝軍將鍇廷蔡迎歡

November 24, 1934. Delta Chinese gather in Locke to honor General Tsai Ting-kai (center, left), Commander of the Republic of China's 19th Route Army, defender of Shanghai against the 1932 Japanese invasion. General Tsai's worldwide tour took him to Belgium, Czechoslovakia, France, Switzerland, and major cities in the United States as well as the Delta Chinese communities of Isleton, Courtland, Walnut Grove, and Locke. (Photo courtesy of Bob Jang.)

land too. There was a big meeting where all the Chinese school, we went over to Stockton to get the uniform, and we all have a big parade in back, where the vegetable garden is; we build a big platform there, behind the old man's home there. Everybody came up and helped build that platform, all three cities—Courtland, Walnut Grove, Isleton—people from the ranches all came up, and we had a big banquet too that day. And all the schoolchildren watched with their banners, and I took care of the Chinese school, the children's uniform: the boys all wear a little top sweater, blue trousers, and have a little whatchacallit, the cap, the army cap that comes up, something like a skull cap.

People were so poor—a dollar a day, Depresssion, no money, those that have a little all contribute quite a bit to him too. He came with his interpreter, a graduate of either Harvard or Princeton—in fact, Columbia. He was very interested in me because I could speak English and know so much about China for America-

民族英雄

歡迎 GEN. TSAI TING KAI 蔡將軍 歡迎

譽名軍

一月廿四日美國加省樂居汪古魯埃崙頡三埠聯

born first generation; very few people know too much about China. I was so interested in geography.

There was such a feeling of unity, and patriotism too. At that time, Chinese are very patriotic. And they're also raising funds for the rice bowl—one bowl of rice [the Bowl of Rice Campaign, to raise money for Chinese refugees during the Sino-Japanese War]. That was in the Depression too, one bowl of rice, San Francisco, all over the United States, and so was our little small town. So I was in a committee too, with a few ranchers, you know, to go to all families and ask for donations to send back to China for the refugees. I forgot which year that was. All over the U.S. the Chinese community all donated for this. It was in the thirties, I think . . .

What held the town together? Well, let's say there's two business people get together and they need English, so I come along. And then if anything happens, like for instance, buying the fire truck, then we all put in our

suggestion—the merchants, the business people, those are people that are financially able to cough up the money first, you know. They come together, all townspeople, those that are able to come out and do something anyway. And sometimes they need me [as an interpreter], I come along too. And then they would put out little rules; somebody will be a secretary and put down the rules, and then how to go about it, and then each place—each family or each house—donate so much: Big Street—Main Street—puts a little more; Second Street—Key Street—a little less. Pretty fair, isn't it? They also put out money for that big pump too, that water pump. Gambling house put out more, because they generate more money. They're very good as far as doing community work.

Ping's [Lee] father was very interested in politics. He was the man financially and spiritually very supportive of Dr. Sun. He was a regular revolutionary. I know auntie was telling me that. Even Ping's father always tells me about the old stories. I'm a good listener, that's why they love me so much. They're very good people; very community-minded. Very generous, have a lot of compassion. At that time we were so poor, during Thanksgiving, Uncle-—I call Ping's father Uncle—at that time my husband is away, it was bad times, so he would roast a turkey, ask my boys to go over there, give us gravy, we cook our own rice at home: we have turkey, gravy, and sometimes sweet potato, and vegetable. He's the only family that cared for us. During the time I told you we were so poor then, they were up in Grass Valley. So years later when times wasn't good either, they moved back. And then we dealt with things together. I often remember being taken care of by them. They were my benefactors.

We didn't really celebrate anything, because we're so poor. We didn't celebrate our anniversary. And then Christmas we don't celebrate, except we have a little church there, a little missionary church, we go there once a year. The only recreation we have is that church. Community things is when Chinese have their holidays—New Year's. Each individual household. We'd eat, most kinds of food. And then sometimes your friends from the ranch would come and see you for New Year's. My house is the big meeting place, because I subscribe to a newspaper, I listen to radio—an American newspaper, a Chinese newspaper too. At that time, I had the *San Francisco Examiner*. When I was first married my husband subscribed to it, coming through the RR—the rural route—coming every day. I'm very much informed for a Chinese at that time. I'm interested. But finally when times are bad, I have to stop the subscription.

One time I went out to San Francisco for a banquet with my uncle, Wah Lee, and so we went on the riverboat, the Delta Queen, to San Francisco. And we walk down to Walnut Grove to get on it. And then it doesn't leave until about ten o'clock. You can hear it. First thing, when they're coming down from Courtland

you can hear the WOOOOOOO! That horn, you know, coming all the way down, they have the bridge open up, see. So, it's an overnight trip. We sit on the benches the whole night, that's all. They do have state—what do you call them? Staterooms—but they have sitting rooms inside, enclosed. We sat there. I think it was a dollar or something, or two dollars, something like that, I've forgotten . . . It wasn't too much fun. It was nice to get away though. See, my folks is in San Francisco, my parents lived there. I didn't see my parents too often. My father and mother never came up, not until years later my father had a vacation. And that was by bus, about ten, fifteen years later. He didn't come up more often because of his financial situation.

We got into San Francisco about six in the morning. And we come home on that too, you know. A lot of Chinese used it as a mode of transportation if they're able to . . . We also had a train coming down from Sacramento, and stop in Locke and we get our mails there too. I remember once, I went up to Sacramento, I went to a hairdresser and they wouldn't take me. I walked into the shop, and when they see that you're an Oriental, they just ignore you. So at that time I realize that, and I walk out. Another time, coming down here in '42, I went to Bullock's there, those salesladies even ignore you. I would just walk away, wouldn't even say nothing. The Chinese, we're good at that; we don't make a big loud noise about it. But now— yes! The present generation they do. They can assert themselves. We don't, you know. When you see they didn't want to attend to you, why you just walk away, do something else. My husband said . . . well, he didn't go to white areas too much. They always go to San Francisco and wander in Chinatown, then you don't meet those discriminations too much, unless you go into a place where more people are Caucasians. And then when we go to take our vacations or big places, it's mostly our own people, you see, so we don't have much to do with them.

I was in Locke then, and I came down here in '42. That was the start of the Second World War. My cousin bought this restaurant here, and was conscripted in the army. He had it only two months, he hate to give it up, because at that time the Japanese all went to their detention camps, and he took it over. So I went down and run the place for him. I always say, "I come, see, and conquer," you know, just like Julius

Riverboat, Sacramento River. *Stern-wheel and side-wheel steamboats plied the waterways of the Sacramento River Delta between San Francisco, Stockton, and Sacramento, hauling goods, passengers, and mail. Chinese laborers paid for passage beneath the bow in what was called the "China hold." (La Vern Studios/Frank Cowsert)*

Caesar. Ha ha! I told him I'll come down and take a look. If I can manage it, I'll manage it, but if not, I'm going home. So I came down, I liked it. Everything worked out and my husband came down, my children came down. My children have been down here in L.A. longer than I was up in Locke . . .

My ambitions for my children were that if they were smart enough, they should go to school and go to college too. But at that time, the war kind of interrupted, the Second World War. My oldest son went into service over in Europe, in the army, in the hospital corp. He was so scared. You know, our Chinese children never go out; he'd never been away from home. So he's just eighteen he was conscripted—went clear to Texas, to Abilene. It was so cold; in California, you don't get ice sticking on there. See, my children, at that time we were so poor, the furthest place they go is San Francisco, that's all. They didn't even have a chance to go to Sacramento. Finally, he came back, he was discharged in New York. He went to school on the GI Bill—he took up photography. So he came back, but you couldn't make your living from photography then.

I had four restaurant then, and I put him to work in them. He was green too, I taught him how and he ran one. When we moved down here my husband came and helped in the restaurants. Then after, when I closed up my restaurant, he went to work with a furniture place downtown . . . I have nine grandchildren now. One great-grandchild. Chinese go for big families. Just like in China, when they congrat-ulate you, it's wealth and children. Nothing else. Children first, and wealth. If you have children, you are wealthy. You know, you understand their philosophy?

I came down to L.A. in February, '42, and I went home in June for my second son's graduation. After that, no, I don't go back to Locke. The last time I went up was about three years ago, to see my sister-in-law. The town was pretty sleepy, depressed. People moved away, and your friends are gone. The people lived there all moved. I go to see Everett's mother, and then I used to know, right across the street, Mr. Ng. He was friends with my husband . . .

I hear Locke's going to be a state historical town; they've been talking about it for the past ten years. Well, they better do it fast, because otherwise it's going to deteriorate, don't you think it will? That's what I'm afraid of. And then people that live there, if they have the town in mind, they should have cleaned up the place, and paint up the buildings, and give it a little fresh start. But I know that I wouldn't go back there. It's a nice town to live, but as a second home. If you like fishing, things like that. Because otherwise, there's no other things for recreation, except when you went boating. For me, I don't like outdoor things, I don't care to go back. I don't fish. I won't be going back. See, my auntie's gone. No matter how hard it was, we always went back and say hello to her, and see her, so now she's gone and I don't think I'll ever go back there. And all my friends, all gone; either they died or left the place. And their children all are scattered . . .

Jo Lung in front of his home, Levee Street, 1986. "I eat rice, I eat fish, I eat vegetables, I eat good things. I cook for myself, and drink whiskey a little bit. You want to walk, you want to exercise, you want to keep your body strong. If you don't walk, then no more, no more walk. People should live to 200, 300 years old. I die 150, maybe 200 years old . . ."

Jo Lung

Jo Lung lives on Levee Street in Locke, in a rundown wooden house he shares with several of the town's stray dogs. The father of three daughters, all of whom have left Locke, "Lung Bak" (Uncle Lung), as he is affectionately known in Locke, is an active part of the town's current Chinese population. He maintains a plot in the community gardens behind the town, visits frequently with his neighbors, and can be found after mealtimes walking determinedly through town with the aid of his cane—and oftentimes a shot of whiskey. Like many Chinese of his generation, Mr. Lung was preceded to the Golden Mountain by his father, who came as a railroad worker. Jo Lung started out as a Delta farm laborer and eventually worked his way up to field superintendent, overseeing crews of Filipino orchard workers for labor boss Charlie Lee Bing. The added income allowed him both to raise a family and to pursue two of Locke's principal diversions—gambling and drinking. Each time we see him he appears visibly more saddened by the town's deterioration, and the deaths of his contemporaries. Nevertheless, as he nears eighty, Lung Bak remains a wry and humorous raconteur.

Jo Lung alternated between English and Chinese during the interviews.

CHARLIE BING? Sure, I worked for him for a long time. I worked outside, then come back, Charlie Bing, he get my money over at the gambling house. I worked in Rio Vista, doing irrigation, then I was a boss over at the camps a long time ago. Had forty men under me. Filipinos, not Chinese . . . I worked in the orchards, asparagus too . . .

China, here, all the same, no difference. You work hard over here, too. You work and toil for maybe ten, twelve hours a day over here. The pay was seventy-five cents a day, for a ten-hour day. Seventy-five cents to a dollar. Whether you like it or not didn't matter. You do the job and you have to do it no matter what. A job is a job. My father was over here, also seventy-five cents a day, working the railroads. Building railroads was a lot harder than orchard work. It was hard work back in those days. Now it's so much easier—machines and everything to help you do your work.

You lived in the camp. Eat boss's food and chow chow for your seventy-five cents a day. The food was pretty good. Rice, fish, vegetables. Three meals a day and the boss give you food, chow chow, and seventy-five cents a day. Twenty-five, thirty men, we all ate together. They'd give you a bed, too, houses for the workers. Everybody had a cot, and all you had to do was bring a blanket or whatever you needed to sleep.

Everything was cheap back then. It was

cheap to go buy groceries. You could go buy ten cents' worth of pork. I go to Hun Hop and say, "Hun Hop, I want ten cents worth of pork." Today you say you want ten cents' worth of pork they say you crazy, get out. Ten cents, twenty cents for half a pound of pork. If you want a half side of beef, seventy-five cents a pound. There was a slaughter house right over there [to Motlow], near your mamma's garden there. They raised the pigs and killed them whenever they needed it. It didn't have to be frozen or anything. Fresh . . .

The wage was the same. White, Filipinos, Chinese—everybody make the same back then. Some people had no chow chow, no eat. I remember some of the Americans, white people, looking for work. Had a blanket wrapped around them, they'd go from house to house looking for work. They'd ask if they could chop wood and then they'd get a piece of bread to eat. These people wanted to work but there was no work so they'd go from place to place and ask people if they'd give them some work to do. The white people would say if you chop some firewood for me, I'll give you something to eat. So they'd chop some wood and come back and they'd give them just a few pieces of bread, that's all.

I hardly ever stayed here. We made some money and I'd go to San Francisco and watch movies. They had Chinese shows back in those times, operas and movies, and we'd go watch them. You could take the bus down, or the boats. The boats would be parked right up there [points to nearby wharf on the Sacramento River]. Paddle boats. Cost seventy-five cents to go to San Francisco. It was a day's wages, but everything else was cheap back then. They used the boats to take everything down to San Francisco—people, pears, squashes, everything . . .

I go to bars. Whiskey all the time—whiskey, wine, beer. My wife used to tell me, "Oh, your body has too much alcohol, too much" . . . I'd go everywhere and gamble too. I go to

Isleton, Walnut Grove, Sacramento, everywhere. I liked to play. And I win a little bit, too, playing dominoes. Every night, day and night, people came to the gambling houses. All Chinese. Before there were lots of Chinese people here, over a thousand people in Locke. They came from the camps, the orchards, mostly working people. Now there's no more. Yuen Chong market, there used to be seven or eight people work there before. Now Dustin [Marr] work on his own . . .

Opium, yeah, back then there was some. But now, no more. No more smoking opium . . . You used to buy it, go to your own room. You sniff, sniff—you smoke this way . . . you go to your own room and smoke it, no special building for it . . .

[The following part of the oral history took place inside of the Dai Loy Museum, Main Street, Locke, formerly Charlie Lee Bing's principal gambling hall. The words Dai Loy stand for "a very big welcome."]

You buy your lottery ticket here. One person inside, usually Charlie Bing. He sells tickets. The man inside spoke Chinese, he'd sell tickets, then sing his little song while he opened up the ticket [Jo Lung calls out lottery numbers in a sing-song voice].

Yeah, I liked to win, liked to win money. But oh crazy head! Charlie Bing, he get your money. You lose, you don't win. You have no more money, you go to work again. You have payday, you come gamble again.

There were one, two, three—three gambling houses in town. The sheriff around here was in Courtland—Goodman. Goodman, one time he said, "I'm going to catch you gambling houses. One year I catch you two times and you better watch it." So, the gambling houses had people who sat outside, watchmen who sat outside and watched for the police. Police come, they lock all the doors. When police leave, they can open up again.

I remember one day this Hindu man comes up to the gambling house, he's got a

Portrait of Ow Hoy Kee, 1979. *"Hoy Kee worked in a gambling house. He was a handsome guy when he was young—tall, you know. He'd come up to my father's place about seven o'clock after work, and in those young days he'd be there until about midnight. Then he'd go home and go to work and be back all over town the next night. Hoy Kee went all over for my father: Weed, Shasta City, Susanville, Chester, Plymouth County, and he wound up in Locke. My father was very fond of him."—Ping Lee.*

turban, a towel, wrapped around his head. Just a Hindu guy, and he drinks too. So the Hindu guy goes, "me Hindu, let me inside." The watchman thinks he's just a Hindu guy, he can go inside. So, he goes inside. Once he goes inside he looks at everything. He takes off to the bar and orders a drink, looks around at everybody gambling. Then he takes off his towel and everybody turn around—and it was Goodman!

"What's he doing in the gambling house?" Oh, that Goodman, he caught them good. He caught them and they set bail. Cost them a thousand dollars. But he doesn't bother the boys or the workers. He wants the boss. He bothers the boss. Charlie, everybody. But money talks—you got the money, all right, you can go . . .

I have three daughters. Locke is an old town and they don't like it—what would they do in Locke? One works in Sacramento. She's a secretary at the Capitol. Another one's married, a housewife. The third one just graduated from college in Sacramento. That's a good town. The young people don't like Lockee. They're all gone. Only the old stay here. But most of the old ones have died. There are only a few Chinese here now, maybe twenty. Just old men here now. Hoy Kee and me. I'm seventy-six, Hoy Kee eighty-nine.

[Strikes a Kung Fu pose] But I'm pretty lively now. See?

Translated from the Chinese by Connie Chan

Ng So Yung

Born in the village of Dung, Zhongshan County, in 1897, Ng So Yung left China and his family farm for Mexico in 1920. He worked for a year and a half in Mexicali as a cotton picker, then paid to have himself smuggled into California. Arriving by ship in San Francisco, he was taken by a cousin up to the Delta, where he went to work immediately in the orchards. Bright, ambitious, and extremely energetic, Mr. So Yung put his farming experience to work during the Depression by forming a tenant partnership with another Chinese, eventually increasing the crop yield of pear orchards under his care nearly 80 percent. In 1957, at the age of sixty, So Yung returned to China to get married. The following year his wife joined him in the Delta. By the time he retired from farm work and settled in Locke, So Yung's wife had borne two daughters and a son, all of whom eventually went to college. Because of declining health, Ng So Yung left Locke in 1984 to join one of his daughters and her family in Sacramento. This interview was done by Todd Carrel as part of the work on his documentary film, American Chinatown. *It is reprinted here with his permission.*

OUR WAGES WERE TWO dollars an hour—no, no! Two dollars a day! The whites treated us Chinese like slaves. After World War II everybody became good friends, but before that we yellow-colored people were considered inferior. I did the work, I didn't cause any problems. I ran a restaurant for a while, but mostly did farm work. I picked grapes, cherries, pears, all kinds of fruits, all over. Besides that we washed toilets, chopped wood, drained milk, maintained the gardens for their families . . . In the past China was weak. The Chinese government could not protect us. Anybody could kick us whenever they wanted. But now it's different. The Chinese government can protect its people, thanks to what Mao did . . .

Ng So Yung on his porch, Key Street, 1975.

I've lived here for over eighty years now. I certainly do like it. Our Locke is very famous. It was founded by a Chinese—Chan Tin San—in 1912, and inaugurated by Chinese. The whole world knows that Locke is a good place. It's the only Chinatown in California now. There used to be more, but now it's the only one left. That's why they want to keep the history. But if we don't develop here, it's going to become a ghost town. If we have something for the tourist to see it would become a lively place. But now we don't have that much.

A lot of the people are crazy, trying to keep tourists out. They don't want anyone to disturb them. I know what they're thinking: they don't want a lot of noise here. But if they want life to stay quiet they can move to Courtland or Isleton, then nobody'll bother them. But the young people, they don't like it here anyway. They've got no job to do. To be a goddamn farmer—

Interior, Ng So Yung's house, 1975.

how much an hour? Only three dollars an hour! If they worked in the stores in the city they would get eight to nine dollars an hour . . .

[Further interviewing with Ng So Yung by the authors was never completed due to his illness.]

Translated from the Chinese by Todd Carrel and Albert Ting

Roberta Yee

Born Mae Jong in Zhongshan, China, in the 1920s, Roberta Yee came to the Delta in 1930, where she lived with her sharecropping family on a pear farm outside Rio Vista before moving to Locke. Like many of her generation, she shed her Chinese name the better to blend in when she entered American schools. She also changed schools twice in order to flee the pressures of anti-Chinese prejudice in the Delta. A bright and highly sociable woman, Mrs. Yee lives today in a sprawling, farmlike house in Palo Alto, California, where she works as an independent real estate agent and helps run the Chinese Community Center of the Peninsula, which she and her husband founded in 1968. Mr. Yee is a self-employed contractor, providing sales and service for electric carts. Except for occasionally leading an organized tour group to her old home town, Mrs. Yee rarely visits Locke any longer. No one from her family remains there. Her oldest brother is a retired mechanic from Alameda Air Base outside Oakland, while her other brother is a vice president of Merrill, Lynch in Oakland. Parts of this oral history originally appeared in East/West Chinese American Journal *and are reprinted with permission of the* Journal.

WE CALL IT "TAI HAN," or the Big River. When we say we are from Tai Han it could be any of the small towns along the Sacramento River, running from "Yi Fow," #2 city, Sacramento, to "Tai Fow," big city, San Francisco. Along Tai Han there's the small Chinese village we call "Lockee." It may look a bit like a ghost town now, but in her heyday—wow!

My folks, my father was here [in the United States] . . . my *grandfather* was here during the railroad and mining days. Then my father was here at the turn of the century. He was one of those trying to seek a place, he went to Arizona

Roberta Yee in her living room, Palo Alto, 1986.

and up, and finally settled in Winnemucca, Nevada. He was a tailor, making shirts, trading with the Indians. Then he went back to China and got my mother, and when he returned they moved to the Delta and started working in the pear orchards on Grand Island. My second brother was born near Ryde [about five miles downriver from Locke].

Then around 1920 there was a big gang, hatchet-man fight—a tong war in San Francisco. My father was more or less a Christian, he never wanted to belong to any tongs. So the tongs were going to go after him. So he took my two brothers and my mother's nephew—now here's something interesting: his mother was the first Chinese aviatrix. She got killed in Redwood City in a plane crash, that was the early twenties. She was an Owyang, Frances Owyang, born and raised in Locke. She married my mother's first cousin, and somehow both of them died and they left this orphan. So when they went back to China they took these three boys with them.

That's when I was born—when they were in Guangdong. Zhongshan. We came back in 1930, just in time for me to start school. We settled in Locke, of course. Locke was the base. We lived on Main Street temporarily, until we found a ranch, and then we moved to Ryde, about two miles south of the Ryde Hotel. My father went into pear farming. We grew pears, that was the main industry. But besides pears, we had chickens and eggs and other kinds of fruits. So that's why even if we don't have the money, we have all these nutritious foods.

We lived in a house on the ranch. See, at that time, you were either a tenant farmer or a sharecropper. You either split the profit with the owner, or as a tenant, you lease it. The best deal was a sharecropper: you work, and you share the profit with the owner. That's what he did. My father's name is Song—Song Jong. His first cousin, my uncle, is Sing Jong. I just saw him the other day, he's ninety-three, ninety-four, up in Sacramento. He was the only person I knew who could carry a hundred-pound sack with his teeth. He doesn't have any now . . .

My two brothers and I started school at Beaver Union School. When we returned to the Delta in 1930, we went there too. It wasn't like Walnut Grove [i.e. segregated]. It was only Isleton, Walnut Grove, and Courtland that were divided. When we started at Beaver Union we were just a handful of Asians, and it was a good background for me. The teachers were just wonderful. They really *teach* you.

And then my father changed farms. We moved right across [the river] from Clarksburg, and we switched schools. I went to Courtland. They bussed us to Courtland. My brothers started high school in Rio Vista, and then when they went to Courtland it was a great big change. They were really prejudiced there. You can feel when there's discrimination: you don't feel at home, you don't feel comfortable. But instead of griping, they just went and got permission to go to Sacramento High School, because we were living not too far from Sacramento. We "kept our place" in those days, and that's how we got along. I decided to go to Freeport school, a two-room school. I think I was the only Chinese girl. I had already learned to integrate, in Beaver Union, because most of the kids were Portuguese. After that, I went to Courtland High School. It was very strict, the principal was from West Point. That didn't bother me. But if you wanted to be in a school play or something, no way you could participate, because you were Chinese. I think it was the teachers there, the way they choose people. So I told my father, "I want to go Sacramento, I'm gonna get myself a school job and go to Sacramento High School." My senior year, I did. I graduated from there. I integrated and had white friends there right away.

We moved back to Locke when my father retired from farming in the late 1930s. We'd really look forward to the pear season. During the pear season everything would be happening in Locke. The workers would come in from all around; they'd stay on the ranches, and then they'd come into town on weekends. I saw a sign that said "Locke, population 2,500." You just can't imagine, there's so many people there at that time. Every building, every house is occupied. All these people lined up, sitting out on Main Street. Every house had a house full of kids. So you'd go out to Main Street, it was just like Easter Parade. We'd sit on the benches, talking. This town was all for Chinese. The Caucasians go to Al's Place, and once in a while you see Caucasians go into the butcher shop.

The pear season would last about three weeks. City boys usually found jobs in the orchards to pick pears. In the evenings after work

Dorsey Runyan estate, River Road, 1986.
*Chinese sharecroppers and laborers worked
the orchards and fields of this estate and
others in the Delta, living in barracks and
field houses at the back of the property.*

the fellows would stop in town for a pool game or a soda. There would be girls sneaking out to meet them. They would go to a movie in Walnut Grove or drive to Lover's Lane. Some of us would sit on the veranda lined with honeysuckles. We would visit and swat mosquitoes.

I had my first job in Locke, sorting pears in the packing house on the wharf. There used to be three of four packing companies using the large wharf on the levee. You start with the spinach right after the New Year's. That's the first produce that comes in. We worked for thirty cents an hour. Spinach, and then asparagus, and then we started the first crop of cherries, and then the pears. Truckloads of pears would line the dock. After grading and packing, the pears were stored in refrigerated railroad cars, waiting for the long trek back east.

The people here were so industrious. The women tended their vegetable plots in the back of town. Those were beautiful gardens back there. The water tank was located there, and each one carried her own bucket, filling it up

from a common faucet for watering. The bucket served a dual purpose—as a portable latrine, to carry the "night soils" to fertilize the garden. Tending the vegetable gardens was a social activity too, where women got together and participated in a bit of back fence gossip. Other times they would knit, sew, cook, or just chit chat.

Everybody I know in Locke worked hard. Even my mother 'til her old age, she wouldn't want anybody to see her sitting around doing nothing. When she was over here during her last year—she died back in '72—she managed to spend all day long planting. She would be out there all day long, and that was typical. That's why so many people went into gambling. It's easy money. All the people that ran the gambling at that time, the kids are all millionaires now, I would say. There's several families in Sacramento, they're all over. And they're the ones that make the money, and their kids are well off.

Locke was a wide-open town. I remember the gambling joints—I'd go in and take a look. There was a smoke-filled room, oh, it was very active, all these pipes going, all day long, and all night too, way into the deep night, men trying to make an easy dollar. But we avoid those places! If your parents knew you went to one of those places you'd get a good whopping. In the old days, when they'd open a gambling joint, the missionaries would settle right next door! There was a lottery every hour on the hour. When someone won an eight-spot the joint would set off a string of firecrackers. If a nine-spot, a bigger string yet. Lottery winners could win nine hundred, a thousand dollars. Two hundred dollars maybe. Some of us kids would

dash toward the place where the winner happened to be, waiting for a handout, knowing the winners liked to share their luck. Every store had its lottery tickets, you didn't have to go to the gambling halls to buy lottery tickets. Every store except Wah Lee: that's where you got your jeans and shoes and underwear, but I don't think he sold lottery tickets. The drawing of lottery numbers always took place inside the gambling joint.

There was a brothel or two in town too. One was next door to Yuen Chong, and on the side street [Key Street], there was one towards the end. I used to see the white prostitutes walking their dogs and getting a whiff of fresh air themselves. As I recall, they weren't bad looking! Looked out of place though.

Those places weren't meant for the residents. They were for other people who come from out of town, from the farms mostly, and the cities. The family people don't go there to gamble. Maybe it's a few bachelors or single people got nothing to do, they don't go to Sacramento, they go there for a good time . . . we knew some of those men. They're all related. Like when we needed workers on our farm, it's the relatives from Locke that comes and lives with us during the season, and then they move back. You know, upstairs of the buildings, they each have their own bedroom, they rent a little bedroom upstairs and that's their home. And then they go around to different ranches, different seasons. We always hire back the same relatives every year, to pack and pick pears, just like a family then.

When I'd go anywhere I'd go to Lim Kee and Yuen Chong's for the groceries. The other one was Fun Hop—they made the nicest tofu. Oh, delicious. The bread man came every morning to deliver fresh bread, and that bread was so delicious! Ten cents a loaf, it melts in your mouth. It came from Sacramento, on the bakery truck. My mother's relatives were here too. They had that Lim Kee Company. I used to go there and make sodas, milkshakes, and I

Mrs. Lon C. Owyoung in her garden behind Locke, 1985. "*I got my garden like a lot of other people did: the older folks who didn't want their garden anymore would just give it to you. They just gave you the land.*"

used to go behind the counter and serve the people. There were two pool tables there and I used to play pool.

But the school would occupy most of our time. There was Chinese school which we had to attend every night after regular school. And then during weekends we could go to Sacramento and maybe go shopping. And visiting—people would come visit us. And you have studies. There's a lot of homework in those days, not now. I went to church a lot as a kid too; not the church itself, but I'd love to go visit the Baptist missionary [in Locke]. It's just like any church Sunday school, they kept kids busy, working on projects like woodworking. It wasn't all the kids in town, maybe 25 percent of the kids would go . . . I'd play piano for the Sunday school there. There was a Lilian, she used to play that piano, and if nobody else plays I'd play for vesper services. I'd help the Sunday school teachers. I think being involved with the mission helped me, because I still go to church. My father would encourage us to go to church. When he went back to China he started a Chinese school in our village—the Cumberland Presbyterian Church. The missionaries would take us to different churches on different Sundays . . . Fort Bragg, Mendocino County, Sacramento, Stockton, and then we have people visiting us from other places . . .

Then we used to take tubes and tires and go swinging and swimming underneath the dock. Every evening we could hear the Delta King or the Delta Queen churning up the river. I used to stop to listen to the sound of their whistles, first loud and then gradually fading away. It was nostalgic even then, though I don't know why. And the fishing in the back, you know, that slough in the back, you could go fishing there too. A couple of kids got drowned back there . . . I remember one kid, his father owned that Moon Cafe, he got drowned.

We had our night watchman in town, Bing Bak, the "Bok Bok Man." Bak means "uncle," and "bok, bok" is the striking sound on the wooden block. Every night he would walk the town and strike a wooden block according to the time. "Bok!" meant "one o'clock in the morning and all is well. Bok, bok!—two o'clock and all is well," and so on . . . There was old man Pete, the hermit, who lived over the railroads behind the town, along Lover's Lane. His home was an old shack, but his garden was his real joy. We used to go there and look at his flowers, and when no one was looking we'd pick some.

There was a family, the Ows—Ow Wing and Ow Fook—they ran a Chinese stagecoach line up and down the Delta. Everyday, you'd go in the morning, from Courtland to San Francisco and back. It was just a limousine, but enough to furnish all the necessities. We want something from Chinatown, you just give them a note, they'll go buy it and deliver it. It stopped running after the war, when people got their own transportation, and people started moving out from Courtland.

I eventually went to Sacramento Junior College, then to UC Berkeley. I got a BA de-

Roberta Yee (second from right) with friends and neighbors, Key Street, 1938.
(*Photo courtesy of Roberta Yee*)

gree—then I got married. My husband lived in Chinatown [San Francisco]. My first job was working for an import company. But my first full job was working for the Veterans Administration, taking care of benefits accounts. And then I got pregnant. I've got four kids . . . five grandchildren. I've got a daughter and three boys. My daughter and first son were born in Children's Hospital [in San Francisco]. Then we moved down to Texas. Now that was different! My husband was a traveling salesman for China Dry Goods, they imported housewares and things like that . . . My second son was born in Dallas. Then my husband couldn't stand it anymore down there, so we moved back. Went to Menlo Park in '55, and we've lived up here [Palo Alto] since 1971.

My daughter, she's got three kids now. Would you believe she married a black? That really turned my husband off. I hate to say it, it hurt, I was in between. That was the most difficult thing in my life to bear—that I had to be right between them. Then my first son married a white. My second son married a Chinese girl. We have one more to go, he's not married yet. My second son's a CHP [California Highway Patrol], stationed right here in Redwood City.

You know, every child should have a chance to grow up on a farm. Then you know where aches come from, you know how hard people work, where the produce comes from. People really don't know how vegetables are grown, and how foods are grown and packed, and all the work that's put into farming. It's hard work, yet it's a great blessing, I would say. It also unites all the family. Farm people always unite because the families are together a lot of times, instead of breaking up, like nowadays. I mean, this is the deterioration of society, the breaking up of families. That's why if parents take good care of the kids you don't see the kids go off . . . My folks looked after the children. My father would always wake us up for breakfast, and when we'd come home from school dinner was all ready for us. He took good care of us. He was a good cook . . .

My parents moved out of Locke in '46, first to Isleton, then to Berkeley. My father followed my brother, because the Chinese like to go with the son; my first brother wasn't married, but the second brother was married, so that's part of the family. My father died young, in 1949. He died of an aneurysm, I think from all that hard work.

You know, looking back, like everything else there's good and bad to living in Locke. Just like Chinatown now, as my daughter would say, Locke is nothing but a slum and a ghetto, really. The way Chinatown is right now in San Francisco, it was the same thing in Locke. But what else did we have at that time? This was our life. I think the fact that my parents were caring people, it helped me. We're taken care of by our parents, so we have no worries, no problems. Our problems were very small compared with what our parents carried through life.

Jone Ho Leong

In her straw hat and black pajamas, a hoe on her shoulder and bucket in hand, Jone Ho, seen in profile in the morning light on the way to her garden plot, is as archetypal a sight in Locke as the sunrise itself. An intelligent, feisty, opinionated woman, Jone Ho is the daughter of Zhongshan farmers who made a go of it as merchants in Australia. By arrangement of her family, she married a Gold Mountain boy in China—a man who returns temporarily after working in the United States. (Her husband, Lai Fong, was the brother of Effie Lai's husband, Lai Foong. He entered the United States under the assumed name of Chong Leong.) But rather than return to the United States immediately, Jone Ho and her husband bought land in Zhongshan district and started farming. For reasons unexplained, Chong Leong eventually returned to America to work in the Sacramento Delta. In 1940, Jone Ho fled the Japanese invasion of China, and joined him in Locke, where she found farm labor work plentiful during the war and postwar boom years. An avid fisherwoman, indefatigable gardener, and willing conversationalist, she considers the success of her two sons, Everett and Daniel, among her proudest accomplishments in the Golden Mountain. Everett currently is the chief of Translation Service for the California Department of Social Services (see p. 121). Daniel lives in Sacramento, where he works as a printer for the California State Employees Union. He and his wife have six children.

I HAD AN UNCLE WHO came back from the United States after working here for two years or so. He came back telling stories how after a day's work you could get out your handkerchief and ring out a bucketful of sweat because of the hard work you had to do. And I remember saying to him, "OK, you can come back here to stay and send us—the women—over there to work. We'll see how we make out over there in the Golden Mountain."

Well, when I got here, after a couple of weeks I said to myself, "If I had $300 I'd go back to China right now." Everything was in shambles. The houses were very rundown: windows were broken, chairs broken, everything was a mess. There weren't any heaters or any conveniences whatsoever. The best thing, the grandest thing that we had was a tea kettle! But if I had gone back to China then, I don't think I would have lived through it. The Jap-

Jone Ho Leong on her porch, Key Street, 1980.

anese were invading, and life was incredibly hard in China. I remember one incident before I left: I was on the bus from Zhongshan to Omun [Macao]. It was during the Japanese invasion and the Japanese airplanes were flying overhead, guns were going off, bombs going off, and I noticed during the bus ride that the guns were getting very close. So everybody on the bus jumped out into a ditch nearby—and the Japanese actually blew up the bus!

I really don't like to talk about the times back then because they were so hard. It's hard for me to relate back to that time, and it's only because James [Motlow] is my friend and I trust him that I'm doing this. Otherwise, I wouldn't do it at all,

I arrived here in 1940. I was thirty years old. Like I said, the Japanese were invading us, so that's when my husband decided to file the papers for me to come. He'd been here for about eleven years already . . .

The trip over here was very hard. I think the most I had with me was maybe two pieces of luggage and some blankets, and that was it. I came by ship, and they kept me on Angel Island for almost two months. Ship after ship was taken into Angel Island, and there were hundreds of people on them . . . I remember people were crying because they were being sent back, and I almost had to go back to China. When the officials asked you questions about work and every other thing, if you didn't answer them correctly you would be sent back almost immediately. I can remember all the crying and screaming going on. There were so many questions to go through, it seemed like I went from interview to interview for the whole two months. It was very hard back in those days . . .

Then after they let me go off Angel Island, I went to San Francisco and stayed for a week with my husband there. Then we came up here to the Delta. My husband was getting a dollar seventy-five a day trimming the branches off the fruit trees in the orchards. Within a week, I

Jone Ho planting garlic in her garden, 1973. "This field back here was full of weeds, and Clay Locke, the owner of the town, was happy when some of us went and asked him if we could plot our gardens out here. We had to set up our own watering system, but other than that there was no problem getting the land. We didn't even have to pay rent at the time, just [for] the water—about five dollars a month. I've had our garden for about forty years now and I'm very grateful to have it and not have to pay rent for the land until now."

was in the street selling asparagus. We worked every day until late . . . we didn't even notice when the sun rose or when the day fell. The work was hard and the wages were low, but there was plenty of work to go around. I was just lucky I wasn't one of those people who spent money the minute I got it. I was able to save up some, and that's what you had to do back then.

My cousins here found me work sorting and packing asparagus. Even the children in the area went to work sorting and packing asparagus. I was paid ten cents for a box of asparagus. The most you could make for a day's work was two dollars. We went everywhere looking for work. We worked in Lodi, in Isleton, even Ryde, anywhere we could find work. We even went as far as Antioch. I also worked picking pears, tomatoes, cutting and packing celery. I didn't know how to speak English. At the canneries we had problems with the floor ladies—the floor attendants—because we didn't know how to speak any English. So if something happened, some problem or something, we would get blamed for it, and we couldn't even argue back.

Like I said, if it wasn't for the war, I probably would have gone straight back home to China. I was from Zhongshan, near Four Districts [Sze Yap]. It's also where Dr. Sun Yat-Sen,

the president of China, was born. Our district was about two hours away from the actual place where Sun Yat-Sen was born. My father and mother were back in Aozhou [Australia], where my father was in business. He had some shops and markets, everything he needed. I had friends back there [in China], I had my own house and farm where we raised pigs and cows and other things, whereas here I had to work in the canneries and packing sheds. But I'd really rather not get into why my husband decided to come to the United States, instead of joining my father's business. It was mainly because of the distance to Aozhou. Other than that I really don't want to get into it . . .

Around 1942 or so the wages started to go up. For the men wages went up to about two dollars a day for picking pears, that type of work. After the season, in November, December, we would go out and prune the trees. Work was cheap, but then, the cost of living was low too. We were living with one of my cousins, who had just bought a place for only five dollars! About two years later I had my first son. I lived there for a couple more years, and then we went up to the Main Street, up on River Road a block, and bought some rooms up there. The house was ours, though the land wasn't; it's their right [the Locke Estate] to do with it what they want. But I was grateful just to have the house. Eventually we rented out rooms to other workers, at the time for only a dollar seventy-five a month, which included electricity and water.

The town [Locke] was very lively back then. Things were really exciting. Most of the people living here were Chinese, with their families and relatives. There were very few Caucasians. As you know, there were gambling houses on Main Street, and on Saturdays and Sundays thousands of people would come into town. Workers on their day off, and other visitors from San Francisco and places like that, they would come here for the gambling houses, mostly.

Jone Ho Leong with her sons Everett (right) and Daniel, 1943. *Mrs. Leong was working ten-hour shifts in a fruit-packing shed at the time. (Photo courtesy of Jone Ho Leong)*

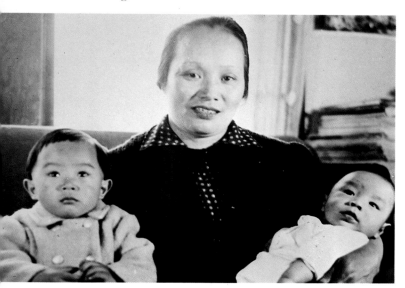

And there were children all over the place. Each family had maybe three or four children, but when I arrived here most of the children were well over ten years old, and my own two kids were the youngest ones in town. The other mothers had to work like I did, but they didn't have to leave their children. They [their children] were able to help their families in working and putting food on the table. Just to give you an idea of how many chidlren there were in town, my aunt next door had five, I had a friend who lived up on Main Street who had ten. There were others in the area with families of four, five, even six kids, so they were able to help out the family when they grew up. Most of the children here did go to school—Chinese school. They learned Chinese, they didn't learn English. When the kids got out of school, they would spend the summers, all of them would go up and help tie or pack asparagus, that type of work, working with their parents.

Like I said, work was cheap, but the cost of living was low, so everything kind of balanced out. You could get a doughnut or a piece of pastry for about five cents. And a favorite for a lot of kids were pig's feet, which you could usually get for about three cents a pound—that's really low compared to now. I remember too, there was a restaurant underneath Joe Chow's house there. When I had company over for dinner my husband used to go over to the restaurant and he'd be able to get a big bowl, plenty of food, things like liver, cow stomach, and bamboo shoots—things like that, which were very popular—for only thirty cents. And that was enough to fill everybody at the house. The main reason chicken and meat and other things were so cheap at the restaurants was, we had a slaughterhouse back where the gardens are, a pig slaughtering house. The Americans usually took the best meat, and our people would go in and take the intestines, all the remainders that the Americans left behind, to use in their cooking. That kind of meat was plentiful because nobody else wanted it. The restaurant owners would trade off maybe a bottle of wine for meat, for the intestines and that kind of thing, so it was pretty cheap . . . I remember one time talking to a relative of mine, my next door neighbor in fact, and saying, "What am I going to have for dinner?" And he answered "Just give me ten cents and I'll go up and get you a big bowl of food at the restaurant."

I said to him, "How can you get something like that for ten cents?"

And sure enough, he came back with *two*

Jone Ho (reflection in mirror) surrounded by family photo gallery, 1973. *"I really don't know about how people's lives have changed around here. My life has always been in looking after myself and my family, just as everyone else's has. I've mainly stuck to myself and worried about my own problems."*

big bowls of a chop suey type of thing—with potatoes and onions and pork, stuff like that. I actually couldn't eat it all . . .

But you know, I've been though a lot of hard times here. I've gone through a lot of jobs and different types of situations, but probably the hardest thing that ever happened was when my two sons, Everett and Dan, were born. At the age of two or so I had to leave them alone. I was working in a cannery in Isleton and they'd hired a caretaker for the children, so I left my two sons with them. My youngest son, Dan, was just constantly crying. It was hard for me to see that, but at the same time I had to go to work in order to support the family and put food on the table . . .

I remember there was a cook for the workers at the cannery there, and he used to say every time I left my two children how insensitive I was, and how uncaring a mother I was to the kids because I left them there crying. But what he didn't know was what I had to go through in order to leave those kids. Those were times when every family had to take care of their own. The government wasn't there with Social Security and pensions, things like that—at least not for us. That was probably the hardest thing I ever did.

Every penny that came to our family was through the work of our own hands. Then in 1950, my husband hurt his arm in the cannery. The doctor said he wasn't going to be able to work, so I worked by myself to support the family. When my husband did get some kind of governmental help, it was from Social Security, not welfare or anything like that. It started at thirty-three dollars a month, and was eventually raised to eighty dollars a month. It was Social Security from the money he worked for himself, not welfare. It was just before it was raised to eighty dollars that my husband died.

I never got a penny from the government, although I had the opportunity to. My friends kept telling me to apply for government money, but I didn't want to because for one thing, the money wasn't much. I figured I could probably make more working by myself. I also wanted to work with my own two hands to be able to support my family. I just felt that I should work on my own. I have been ever since. Even today, the only thing I'm getting is Social Security. And that's all I need.

I worked by myself until Everett, my oldest son, was twelve years old and could finally help me. The manager said he was too small to pick pears, so he told him to go packing pears and making boxes, that type of work. That's what both my sons did after school was out. My main hope for them was to grow up and somehow help the family put food on the table and be able to work beside me. I remember when they were younger, my oldest son used to take care of the house and sometimes he would be doing his homework; but mostly it was to go to work and help support the family. When my kids were about twelve they started going out to work with me in the orchards, picking fruit or sorting pears. They would work all through the summer until school started again. With my own two hands and with the help of my sons I was able to put both of my sons through college.

I've been through a lot, but it's been a fairly good life for me. I was just happy that I could work. I was just very lucky that I was able to work and didn't starve to death over here . . .

It's a quiet life here. I spend my time going fishing or reading the newspaper, maybe going visiting. Most of the time the most I go out is to see your mother [to translator], to visit with her. Other than that I really don't go out much except once in a while to my garden. Most of the people around here keep to themselves, and that's what I tend to do. It would be nice to have more Chinese people here, but where are you going to get them from? They would have to be quite sedentary to live in Locke. They couldn't be the type who want to go out and have fun all the time, because there's just not

that much to do around here . . . It's awfully good for retired people, though, for old people like myself. I'd rather live here than anywhere else, like in the big cities. Whenever I go to see my sons and my grandchildren, after a day or so I'd rather come back here, to my own house. I don't like to go up to the big cities anymore. It's easier for my sons and their children to come down and see me just like they did on Mother's Day, when the whole gang was over. And now that I'm older, I have no desire to go back to China, because there's nothing back there for me. My parents and my family property is gone. There is absolutely nothing for me to go back for. Here, I have freedom to go in and out of my own house. I can go to the

Chong Leong (Lai Fong), Key Street, 1973.
Mr. Leong died on December 8, 1974.

garden whenever I want. I can go visiting whenever I want. If I was in the city I would be staying inside the whole time, because I would be afraid to go out.

I've settled down here in my own house and raised my family. I'm very satisfied with my life.

Translated from the Chinese by Connie Chan

Tommy J. King, 1975. *Due to changing farm labor practices and the lure of nearby cities and universities, only three others of Tommy's generation remain in Locke. The oldest of six children, he stayed in Locke with his wife, Connie, to care for his aging parents.*

Tommy J. King

If Ping Lee is the honorary mayor of Locke, Tommy King, seventy-three, is its watchman, fireman and ombudsman. From his house at the intersection of Key and Levee Streets he can see most of Locke's backstreet traffic, and working eight or nine hours in his garden during the spring and summer, he keeps an eye out on the town where he has lived since 1928. Retired as a radio repairman and electrical technician, Tommy has wired his garden with speakers, and on summer days the big-band sounds and golden oldies from Sacramento radio stations KXOA or KGMS float on the warm river breezes. Besides Ping Lee and his wife, Tommy and his wife, Connie King, are two of only a handful of American-born Chinese of their generation to stay in Locke. As he says pointedly several times in his story, he didn't plan it that way.

Most summer days at flood tide you can find him rowing his little rubber raft in the sloughs behind town, bound for an hour or two at his favorite fishing hole. Other days he rides his bicycle. A shy, intelligent man, Tommy has an abrupt manner of speech which is often laced with irony as dry as a Delta summer day. We spent more than one summer afternoon seated with him in the shadow of his plum tree, the nostalgic tunes of KXOA serenading us from speakers mounted on the side of his tool shed, or in his radio room indoors, where he converses in Morse Code with ham operators around the world.

MY GRANDDAD WAS ONE of the few Chinese here that could speak English. That's why my name is "King." Any time anybody have a business transaction, my granddad was the interpreter. So they call him "King." That's what my mother said. The name just came passed on. That's why my middle name is "Jo"—that's my real name. I think Tommy was the name my landlord gave me. My Chinese name is Chong. My family called me Chong—Chong Jo. People here use all kinds of names. You got a name when you're born, got a name when you go to school, got a name when you got married. That's just the Chinese way of doing it . . .

My father was born in Courtland, I think. His dad came over during the railroad era, then he got married over here and his family was born here [in the Delta]. There's four brothers [points to portraits on the wall of his radio room]. This one never got married. He was way ahead of us—he was living with a woman! He lived with her many years, many women, too, probably. He didn't have a long life. He was the first of them to die.

Sometime before 1910 my grandmother took the kids back [to China] to get married.

Two of them did get married, then returned here. My father was the only one of the children who stayed. He was in his early twenties. I think he was a rebel; I don't think he wanted to go back. Later on he went back and got married. My mother was from China, near Canton. It was an arranged marriage. There's damned few love marriages, you know. Unless they really don't want to go through with it for some damned reason, they take what they get. They're taught that way, you know. That's the culture. They're still doing it, [though] they're gettin away from it. They had arranged marriages here in Locke, yeah. Women are pretty weak. Well, I wouldn't say they're weak, but they have no opportunity to go out and earn a living. It's either get married or starve, right? Or carry your parent's resentment if you want to be a rebel. When I was young, fifty to seventy-five percent were arranged marriages. All kinds of situations. They would bring women from China, they would arrange for a wife back in China, they would marry you to a woman from the Delta. In fact, I know quite a few friends my age that went back to China and got themselves a wife. They would usually take a younger woman, an older man take a younger woman, all arranged. Most of them work out. Offhand I can't think of any arranged marriages that didn't work out. Maybe not too happy, but not divorced.

My mother was born in 1885, '86, around there. She came to the United States in her early twenties, I think. She was in San Francisco during the earthquake. She often talked about it . . . Our first house was in Walnut Grove, right next to that Jean Harvie School. We had a very small house. We had six kids in there, and I think that house wasn't more than twenty by thirty, six hundred square feet. We moved to Locke in 1928, when I was thirteen. The landlord wanted us to farm some open land outside Walnut Grove and my dad didn't want to. My dad was only farming the orchard. He wanted us to take over the open land and farm it, so my

dad quit. We moved into James's [Motlow] mother's place. That's way, way back.

My dad was a rancher for a while, but he quit ranching and went into the amusement business—slot machine business. The gambling business is a way of life, Chinese way of life, you know. He distributed, maintained, slot machines to over fifty places up and down the Delta. He made a few dollars. He also got fined a few times. My dad was a simple man. A very simple man. He had very simple ambitions for us, like being a carpenter or butcher. At one time I think he planned on going back to China. Most Chinese did. One reason he didn't was because of the Japanese war. If it wasn't for the Japanese war I think a lot of families would have gone back. But the main reason is, the Depression broke everybody. The ranchers and the store keepers, it broke them all. In the old days, you know, everything was on credit, like the Caucasian business here now. The only thing, the Chinese only collect once a year—after the crop is in. So when the farmer went broke, the butcher went broke. There was no chance of going back to China. What for, you know? It was still easier to make a living here, rather than go back there and slave for a penny an hour or something like that.

That's my father's garage right there. He kept the slot machines upstairs. He had quite a few. He'd pick them up cargo freight from the Southern Pacific depot in Walnut Grove . . . they came in from Chicago. You know about the gambling houses here, right? Did Ping [Lee] tell you what his father did? Did he tell you his father ran the gambling house in town? Well, Lee Bing never took slots. There weren't any slots in the gambling houses here. They had dice tables, black jack, card games, cater some to the Caucasians—but no slot machines . . . Most of the people played a little. At the peak, there were probably five gambling houses here.

It's a funny thing about Chinese: they know gambling is a bad habit, but they condone it, as a business. When I was a kid my parents told me gambling was a bad habit, like smoking opium. All the Chinese family taught that. A Chinese family is funny, you know. You go to school and you learn the three R's—the first "r" is respect for parents; the second is respect for teacher; the third is respect for the law. See, if you follow that you'll grow pretty good, right? But look at your schools now! Your students don't have any respect for the teacher. They beat them up and all that, rape them and all that, all doped up, right. Of course, I can't say about the Chinese nowadays. That's my days. I pass it on to my kids. How much they absorb of it, I don't know.

I worked for my father for a while, when I was about sixteen—collecting money. I remember driving from town to town, and going into these places with him and opening up the machines. His take at that time was fifty–fifty— 50 percent for supplying and maintaining the machines. No, he didn't rig them. It was totally random. Probably a lot of machines in Reno don't have a jackpot. It's supposed to be honest in Reno, but who knows? You can rig it. In Reno, let's say your take is 6 percent. All you have to do is play a thousand times and see if you get your 6 percent or not. You try it sometime . . . maybe a hundred times. You put in a hundred nickles, you should get six wins on it . . .

As a kid I used to swim mostly, play cops and robbers. Not up on Main Street. It was too lighted, all the stores, everybody had a light hung out. They had streetlights even then, practically the same poles [as today]. We'd play up on the railroad tracks. Cops and robbers. Climb in and out of cars. A lot of places to hide. In the daytime, we'd play baseball, basketball, football. The playground was right here, back where the gardens are.

This town is an oddity now, but it wasn't an oddity then. We had the four towns, the four Chinese sections—Courtland, Walnut Grove, Locke, and Isleton—and the Chinese stage

Main Street, Locke, ca. 1939. (*Photo courtesy of Russell Ooms*)

running from Courtland on down, hauling passengers and freight. The Gibson line, it died out in the fifties. On weekends the town would be really crowded. People coming in to relax—gamble, eat, drink, visit friends. It wasn't really rowdy. If you saw any drunks it was Caucasians. You'd never see a Chinese lying in the street drunk. But it wasn't a lot; you'd have a couple of speakeasies once in a while, not too bad. There were all kinds of stores here then—dry goods, restaurants, hotels, barbershops. It was the only town built by Chinese still standing in the state of California. The thing different about Locke from the other Chinese towns was a different dialect spoken. Walnut Grove was a different dialect: Sze Yap. When I was a kid I spoke that lingo, just like a native. I lived close to Walnut Grove and play with the Sze yap kids, so I speak that lingo. The difference between the two is the difference between a southern accent and northern accent, only more. I think a northerner can understand a southerner, and vice versa, but we had more difficulty. Same word written, but different sounds. My mother's dialect, I couldn't understand that. This town was Zhongshan. Everybody speak that. There wasn't one Sze Yap in Locke, not a one. Walnut Grove is Sze Yap, and everybody who lived there, either speak it or learned to speak it. Sam Yap is the language in between. When Sam Yap people speak, Zhongshan people understand it, Sze Yap people understand it. That's a pretty dialect. The tone. It sounds good. You go to San Francisco, that's what you hear—Sam Yap. If you go to Hong Kong or Canton, that's what you're going to hear—Sam Yap. Only when you go away from the city into the country, then you find all kinds of dialect. Some of them I can recognize—I can recognize three, possibly four dialect or so. Most of the Chinese can speak two dialects . . .

The markets in town were real good, fresh food, from Sacramento. Yuen Chong and Fun Hop . . . Fun Hop, he had a good business. They carried all the Chinese goods, and he have poultry and fish, Chinese vegetables. The guy was good at it; he don't buy no junk. Everything he'd buy was good stuff. Good vegetables, good meat. He'd go up to Sacramento to a butcher house and pick up what the Chinese want, not what they give him, but what he chooses. You know, like pig stomach and pig's feet. That's very popular. Pig's feet usually used for a woman that had a baby, right afterwards. Every woman eat that. During the pregnancy you use up a lot of calcium, and pig's feet, when you boil it, boil the calcium out and the woman drink it. They cook it with rice vinegar. I got some in my ice box right now. I use it all the time. Invigorating. Cook it with ginger. Give you strength . . .

Then let's see, there was one, two, three, four—five whorehouses in town. I was a teen-ager at that time and my parents never told me anything about them. My parents were just like your parents probably, they don't teach you anything about sex. Ever. We knew about them though. They were open all day, all night too. They weren't any problem. You'd see all kinds coming in and out: Chinese, Filipino, Caucasian, Japanese, whoever would show up. Mostly it was night business. You know, it was farming country, everybody work during the day time. The workers would come into town in a buggy, you know, a horse [drawn buggy]. You never seen one of the ones they used on the ranch: long things, they carry fruit and everything else on it. Everybody climb on it. You never seen that, but there were two water troughs for the horses, here in town. One was right outside Fun Hop's, and one was right outside your mother's house, in that empty spot, that empty space between the houses. Then they graduate to motor trucks.

The Chinese people don't resent them. They know that it's a service, I guess. They're practical people. Over here you have no women in those days. The girls are just growing up, and all the women that come over here are either married, or whores. There are some

Women hanging bok choy from their gardens out to dry, Key Street, 1975.

Chinese whores that come over here, just like any other races. So what are the men folks going to do? It's a service, a needed service. The houses themselves were never run by Chinese. Not in this town. Walnut Grove there was; they had a lot of Chinese women. No whites [whores] in Walnut Grove; all the whites were up here. The Chinese people didn't mind. They don't hide it. I guess you could say they condone it. They just mind their own business. They know that men gotta have sex. I don't know about married men . . .

Yeah, we'd see the women, they'd walk around. We didn't socialize with them, of course. The only time they'd go out was when they absolutely had to. Some of them were dressed pretty scantily, though that didn't happen very often. I remember the Chinese women, they'd look at the prostitute walk by all scantily dressed and they'd say, "Oh boy, look at those goddamned tits." Real big tits, you know. Look at that pair of tits! Chinese women, you know, they're flat-chested. When they see a full-bosomed women, I guess it's something different.

At that time, thirties and forties, it cost two bucks to go to the whorehouse. No, two and a half. When I was in Walnut Grove where they had the Chinese whores, you hear the men talk about it. Two and a half. It wasn't any different than today's men. If you can afford it, you go a little more often. You can't afford it, you gotta beat it. The first two buildings that burnt down, they were whorehouses. Then 312 [Main St.], that building upstairs. Then the building that burned down right beside Dustin's; and Ping Lee's place. There weren't any signs or anything. You don't have to put a sign up when you can hear what's going on . . .

Yeah, there were lots of families in Locke. When I was a kid there were thirty to forty families in Locke, easily. Probably one [baby born] every month. Most of your houses are double stories, right? And a lot of them are half houses, split right in the middle. Every house, every store is a family. When I went to Chinese school [in Walnut Grove], there were at least forty to fifty students. Oriental school was about 150 students. We had the schools, the segregated schools. Not only the Blacks had it. I guess all the landowners around here didn't want their children to be going to school with the Chinese. We were a lower class of people at that time. Us and the Japanese. Of course, the Chinese never expected to stay here. They just wanted to come in and make a bundle and go back. But the opportunities just weren't there. Not like now. Now you can practically get into anything. Just like last night I saw on TV a Chinese man, his name was Wu—he's Secretary of Commerce! [Theodore Wu, Deputy Assistant Secretary for Export Enforcement, Trade Administration, Department of Commerce, appointed February 13, 1982]

Do you know where the Walnut Grove School is right now? The old Oriental [segregated] school was directly across from it. Walnut Grove have its own Chinese school. Every town had its own Chinese school—Isleton have, Courtland have, Locke. If you lived on a ranch, then you don't get a chance to go to school. There wasn't no transportation. We lived on the ranch but it was right close to town, right behind the Jean Harvie School there. The orchard's still there, [though] the trees are dying. The Salisbury ranch. Lord Salisbury. I thought he was a Lord, but that's just his name. Lord.

Chinese school was actually a chore, you know. You got off at four o'clock from English school, and then you go to Chinese school at five o'clock and stay there till eight! In Walnut Grove it was nine—five to nine. You know, parents like to get their money's worth. I went there for a few years. They should've given us just one hour and separated all the classes, we wouldn't mind that stuff so much. But three hours, that's a long time to stay there . . .

I guess my family talked about discrimination. My father, I think he just accepted things like that. There was nothing he could do about it. That's one thing you got to give the Blacks credit for: they're big enough to organize and fight in the courts. That's one thing you've got to give them credit for—a better life for the minorities. The Chinese people did very little fighting that I know of. But I was too damn young, I didn't understand. When I went to segregated school, I thought that's the way it was! You know, you never had anything different. That's when this whole county—not the whole county, but from Sacramento to the Antioch bridge—was populated by Orientals. Chinese and Japanese and Filipino. The Filipinos came very late. Mostly Chinese and Japanese. By my time there was very little hostility with whites. We never had anything like the whites treat the Blacks, that way . . . I went to high school two years and I never witnessed a single fight. High school wasn't segregated by then. I went to Courtland High. They tore it down a few years ago. The only fight you'd see is when Caucasians get drunk and ride around in the car and try to get in trouble. There weren't any gangs or anything. They'd drink and ride around the town and start abusing the Orientals. But they're damned fools, because the Orientals don't fight fair. There's no one-to-one stuff. They gang up on you. And besides, the guy's half drunk and can't fight anyway. So all they do is get a great big beating, not broken bones or anything like that, using chains or bats. Just beat 'em up.

But by the time I grew up it was getting better all the time. I never experienced it. My mother had some trouble in San Francisco, I don't know why. The whites don't like the Chinese for some damned reason. Like you have discrimination right now against the Mexicans, same thing . . . You know, when I look at the Mexican now I damned near see my mother. They live in the poorest goddamned houses, work at the poorest grade of job, for the lowest wages, have a lot of kids in their arms, a bunch of kids. One difference, the Chinese are tidier. You ever been to China? All you see are clothes hanging out. Every village, every house you see clothes hanging out. That's one thing you gotta say about the Chinese, they're clean.

You know, when I was picking pears I was about eighteen or nineteen, I had to take a bath in the chicken house. Not with the chickens, but it was a chicken house. You just carry your own bucket in and wash yourself. But you take the Mexicans today, they're protected by law. You've got to have shower, right. You've got to have screens in the windows. You can't let the mosquitoes in and bite the hell out of them, like they did us. They're protected by law. In a way, they're even better off then we are—I mean, than my dad was. You ought to see some of the old buildings that the Chinese people used to live in on the ranches: just bare building, no inside wall, just the outside wall. No double insulation. They might have a stove, because in

the orchards there's a lot of free wood, but the buildings were really bad. After fifteen or twenty years they're pretty well worn down. Before the machinery, you lived out there year round. Now with the machinery one man can run a ranch practically. Spray by yourself, but in those days—take this ranch for instance, you would have probably three teams of spray wagons, with one driver and two sprayers along the side, and it would take weeks. Right now they'd probably run through the orchard in two days, with an airplane probably a couple of hours. The biggest labor right now in the fruit ranch is pruning. They can't speed that up. But outside that, the year-round stuff is gone.

My first job was ranch work, outside of working for my father. Ten cents an hour, all day, room and board. It was sharecropping all the way around here. Chinese just hire all the labor and do all the work, and then share the profits. You worked for the Chinese who had the lease . . . we worked from six to six. They don't do that anymore. Everybody worked from six to six, two hours of rest and ten hours of work. Long day. Sometimes you worked 10 and a half hours. Most of the pruning crews spoke the same dialects; mostly Zhongshan around here. In fact, I can't think of a ranch that had a Sze Yap boss. The one in charge was usually the one that could speak a little bit of English, like my granddad.

You were glad just to get a job. Depression time, we didn't get too damaged by unemployment around here. There was always a lot of ranch work, but it wasn't a dollar a day. During the Depression it was down to seventy-five cents a day, 1932, '31. We had the poorhouses too. Every town had its poorhouse. Courtland have one, Locke have one, Walnut Grove have one, Isleton have one. Just a place to keep away from the elements . . . just a shell. No kitchen or anything, just beds in a row, like a barracks, six or eight people, sometimes more. They work, but some of the men have vices. If you have vices, you can't keep up with it. Gambling and dope—opium. Cocaine. Morphine. But the thing about the Chinese people, they don't go crazy on the stuff like the Caucasians do. You smoke opium, OK. Have a few sweet dreams, that's it. The Chinese don't go crazy. I never saw anybody from my generation on dope, or messed up by it. The generation before me, a little bit. But not going crazy on it, like the whites . . .

I never finished high school. I only went to tenth grade. I quit because I was stupid. I don't know why, but when I was young I just hated school. I think I had a reason, too. I was always interested in electronics—electronics and mechanics—and the schools had neither one of them. If they had, I think I would have gone through . . . but there wasn't anything that interested me. The only thing I took was woodwork. I'm a practical man more than an intellectual guy. Later on I learn that you can be practical about being intellectual . . .

It took me four years to save $600, then I went to school in San Francisco. In six months the money was gone. I spent six months in San Francisco at the Western College of Radio, on Larkin and O'Farrell. I don't think it's there anymore. They taught me the bare fundamentals . . . at that time, since I didn't finish high school, I was handicapped. I didn't know mathematics and science and chemistry, the things I needed in order to understand electricity, to repair things.

That was 1938. I was twenty-four. Then I came back here and opened up a radio shop. I ran it three or four years before the army got me. Actually, I enlisted in the air force. I was one year in Sacramento, one year in Houston, Texas, two years over in CBI—China-Burma-India. I was a radio mechanic for airplanes and ground vehicles. Then after the war I came back and did the same thing—opened up a radio shop. I did that from '46 to '55. When I first opened my shop, after four years of war there was a lot of work to be done. People still had a lot of radios, TV wasn't in yet. So I made a

living at it. But after a while, a lot of businesses here were gone already. There was only one restaurant left. Two grocery stores. Two gambling houses. One pool hall. I guess it started during the Depression. A lot of Chinese move away during the Depression; they couldn't make any money farming, so they moved to the city. I was the only radio shop around at the time but I still never had enough work to keep me busy. Finally, television killed me off. Couldn't handle television. You know how big a television was in those days—about that big, that wide, weighs a ton. You can't lift it without help, you can't carry it, you can't transport it without help. You can't put up an antenna without help . . . I finally closed down and went to work for the Army Signal Depot. Electronics, repair work. I spent twenty years there, and retired nine years ago. Federal retirement, it was a federal installation . . .

I didn't get married until I was thirty-six. I was brought up during the Depression, you couldn't think of getting married at ten cents an hour. My wife was Zhongshan, from Isleton. It wasn't an arranged marriage. I met her at a New Year's party in Sacramento, dancing. American Legion dance. There were a lot of Chinese vets . . . We had two children, boy and girl. My son is thirty-one. The girl is thirty-five already. I wanted them to get a college education. They did. Well, my daughter didn't. She wanted to be a beautician, so she went to beauty school in Sacramento. Didn't like it. Now she's a jewelry clerk. My son went to UC. He got a bachelor's degree. He's with the Sacramento Housing Development. Actually, I don't know what the hell his job is. Must be some kind of analyst, push a pencil.

I raised them both in Locke. They went to school in Walnut Grove. By that time it was integrated. They also went to the Chinese school. They speak Chinese, but not good. After they're fluent in English they don't want to speak Chinese. You know, like everybody else, you use the language that you can get by in.

Key Street alley, 1976.

They regret it, though. All these Chinese kids that can't speak Chinese now, maybe not tell you, but they regret it. Who wouldn't regret the loss of a language, right? Cripe, when they go to San Francisco, why hell, they're like Caucasians. I go to San Francisco, I feel at home. I don't speak it well, but at least I can go into a restaurant and order anything, or talk to the waitress, or when I go buy something I can speak their language. There's two reasons for them not speaking Chinese. One is, because they're not concentrated anymore. Chinese people used to be concentrated. Every city have its Chinatown, and everybody live there. So, the language is there. Later on, when relations is better, everybody move out. They're scattered, so that all the neighbors are English-speaking. But the main reason for losing it is because it wasn't taught—it's not taught in the home. I don't like my children speaking less Chinese. At least they understand a little bit, like "1, 2, 3, 4," so on and so forth, "hands" and "feet" and all that.

I will say this: if my old folks hadn't have been here, I wouldn't have stayed here. My father died around 1970, I think. My wife knows, I'm no good at dates. At least fifteen years. I would have moved out a long time ago. Moved to Sacramento or somewhere. I did live up there for four years. I was a radio technician. Right now I'm retired so it's not too bad. It's pretty good retirement. I go fishing nearly every day. You got to have activity. But I know that if my old folks weren't here, I wouldn't have stayed. Right after the thirties it [the town] started to decline. There were no opportunities here. The young people went to the cities—San Francisco, Los Angeles, Stockton, Sacramento, Oakland, Berkeley. A lot of the old people tried to go back to China. Not too many made it back though. So they bring their families over here. It's a better life over here, anyway. Those that went back and retired, if they had a chance they all came back. Lots of them, they lost quite a bit, things they bought in the old country, like houses and businesses. Back in the old country, why, you can hardly make a living. You work all day just for your room and board, that's more or less slavery, right? A lot of them just stayed [in the United States], and sent money back there. Everybody sends money back there, like the Mexicans now send money back to Mexico . . .

I don't know much about what's happening to the town. All we hear is rumors. The guy [Ng Tor Tai, owner of the town] never hold a meeting to say, all right, this is what's happening. That new deal, as far as we know, the investor backed out. And then, I don't know . . .

Ideally, I want the state to take over the town. The state's the only one that's not going to make money. Everybody else comes in here is going to make money, right? If they're going to put money in, if they're going to buy it, you've got to expect them to make their normal profit. But the state is different. They don't need to make money. They just want to improve it and let the citizen enjoy it. Once you develop the town, then Locke don't mean anything. I think eventually the state will buy it, because it's already a historical site. When the state come in, you have some kind of regulations. Right now there's no regulation here. Everybody do whatever they want. That's how it's always been. I think the only organization that watch over Locke is probably Sacramento Housing. They were pretty interested in preserving the town. They worked pretty hard at it. Later on the state got interested. And then I think Proposition 13 came along and killed it. And now, I think, the federal deficit is not going to help it. Maybe in five years, if they knock off the deficit.

Like I say, if my dad and mother weren't here, I wouldn't be either. My wife's folks are gone. Our kids are in Sacramento. I'd like to see more people move here that like to stay. I don't like to see people that don't like to stay. People that like to stay will make an investment. People that just want to stay a few months, they just use the town. They aren't going to make any improvements. I like to see older people come in. Not necessarily families, but retired people. [To James Motlow] Like your mother—

But I don't think it's going to happen. The town is dying.

Clarence Chu, general manager and co-owner of Asian Cities Development, 1978. *In 1977, Hong Kong–based Asian Cities purchased the entire town of Locke and 490 surrounding acres. Development plans included preserving Locke's Chinese cultural heritage along with constructing luxury homes behind the town, but they never went through. In 2001, Sacramento County purchased the ten-acre town site and began procedures to subdivide the town and turn ownership of Locke's real estate over to its residents for the first time in history.*

Everett Leong

Born nearby in Lodi, California, and raised in Locke, Everett Leong is Jone Ho Leong's oldest son. Today he lives alone in a comfortable suburbanlike section of Sacramento, and heads the Division of Translation Services, California Department of Social Services. His position is consistent with the astonishing success rate of Chinese in modern American society: by 1970, 56 percent of working Chinese-Americans held white collar jobs, well above the national average. Like most of his Locke contemporaries instilled with the Chinese work ethic, Everett never considered staying in the town once he'd grown up. There weren't any opportunities for a Chinese wishing to get ahead. He also seems determined to rectify the legacy of his parents' farm labor and his own miserable experiences working the fields as a child. He was much more willing than the older Chinese to talk about the inequities of farm work. As a native-born American, of course, he feels more secure than those who first came to America as Paper Sons. Today Everett Leong is as American as they come, with one important distinction: like many of the sons and daughters of Locke we talked to, he wants to balance his American identity with efforts to preserve his links with his Chinese heritage and language.

I WAS BORN OCTOBER 1942. One of the first things I remember about Locke is that it was like an old-country town. To me it's the closest thing to nature, yet you still have your so-called basic necessities, accommodations . . . the town of Locke is the closest thing to a Chinese village back in China, OK? The people were all from the old country, back in China. Most of them were farmers and they came over here and they utilized their farming skills and then, you know, people in the town of Locke actually contributed to the agricultural development of

Everett Leong, outside his mother's house, Key Street, 1976.

the Delta. But in those days we didn't think of Locke as a unique town. We only thought of it as the town that we lived in. We didn't perceive it as a special town, or just being developed by Chinese or anything. We just thought we were part of the Delta coummunity.

Most of the time what we did was, in our younger days before we could work in the orchard, most of us just went out and played around and climbed trees, went out to the river, did a lot of fishing, a lot of rock throwing, catching grasshoppers, shooting birds, and then, you know, catching pigeons and selling them to those old men who wanted to buy them to cook pigeon to make soup with herbs.

And then in those days, too, when I was

about between six and ten, the town had a local gambling hall, and that provided a lot of action. A lot of kids hung around out there. Several of us were shoeshine boys, and we used to stick around there and shine a guy's shoes for fifteen cents a shine. They had a chair out back so you could sit down. Plus there's shade, there used to be a big tree back there—the gambling hall right behind my mom's house, the Dai Loy—Ping Lee's father owned it. I never really went inside when I was a kid. Basically I got as far as the door and the back porch and all that, but we knew that there was a lot of people in there and we knew that there was money in there and that if you stick around there long enough with your shoeshine box, the guy that wins will come out and get a shoe shine for fifteen cents a shine, and he'll tip you twenty-five . . . that was the main gambling hall. But like the Chinese Association next door, they had gambling there, too, during the holidays and all that. They played poker, whatever, but the main gambling hall is the one there now—the Dai Loy Museum . . . I remember Ping Lee's father [Lee Bing]. When I was small I'd see him. He was a very businesslike individual, a business man. He was always well dressed. He always had at least a sports coat and a tie on, something like that. In other words, he did not dress up like the typical farm laborers in town; he was better dressed, more professionally dressed than anyone else. Other people of the town looked upon him as a person of a higher level than themselves, because he was a businessman.

My house was on 2nd Street [Key Street]. My mom still lives there. Prior to that, my cousin lived in that house before their [Effie Lai's] family moved to Los Angeles. There were some kids my age, but the decade before my decade, before my time, there were more kids involved. I would say in my decade there was around about fifteen-twenty kids my age . . . I went to Walnut Grove Elementary and Courtland High School. Walnut Grove was integrated

by my time. The majority of students there were pretty well mixed. It was a combination of Japanese, Chinese, and white, and a few Filipino and a few Mexican and very few Blacks. But in my opinion we all got along fairly well in those days, because the school was small. We started in the kindergarten together, and practically 80 percent of us kids went through for eight years. So you knew one another fairly well, and you also knew your teachers pretty well because there was very little turnover of teachers.

Most of the kids from our town came from parents that were non–English speaking. We were brought up learning to speak the Chinese language. When I started school, my basic language skills were in Chinese. When I went to school, that's where I originally developed my English speaking skills. Sure my parents encouraged me. The time to learn English was in school, you know. But in those days the Joe Shoong School was open too. We had Chinese school after our regular day of school, five days—no, six days a week, because we also had classes on Saturday morning. Practically every kid that was born or brought up in Locke is bilingual today. Which is different from most kids nowadays, who tend to lose their original language . . .

I started working in the orchards when I was about twelve years old, picking pears and hauling boxes. I must have done it for seven or eight summers. In those days they had the small boxes, they weren't using the big bins yet. So most of us, we started picking pears when we were just starting high school, right after we got out of the eighth grade. We used to work ten, twelve hours a day out in the orchard, for ninety cents an hour. The highest it ever got to be when I was working in the fields was two dollars an hour.

I started out as a picker, but then I did other things. Later on when I was in college, I irrigated, I cut blight, I fertilized, I sprayed—everything that has to be done during the sum-

Jone Ho Leong, Everett's mother, preparing dinner for her husband, 1973.

mer months. All I know is that it wasn't an easy life, because now I've had a good taste of it myself, you know, working in the fields. The old folks weren't working anymore. They worked in the orchards before then. My mom was working though. She was working in the packing sheds, cannery, and probably also in the fields—tomatoes and other open field crops . . . I don't think there's anger among any of the parents in those days, in regards to working, say, ten hours out in the fields and then coming home and having to cook for five

or six kids. It was something they had to expect. So an expression of anger, I would say, is not a good description of the situation. It was their way of life: you go out, leave home, say, six in the morning and come home six at night. That's part of your daily life. It was a way of life for them . . . but the older people very seldom talk about their past history. What they know they usually just keep it in themselves.

But my opinion, working in the field is one job that I think anybody who works there is well underpaid. In other words, you work your ass off. You start early in the morning and by eight o'clock you're sweating. When you work in the fields, you do, say, three to four hours of work, and it's equivalent to somebody who's sitting in a building working, say, ten hours a day. You come home, next morning you try to get up at quarter to six, five-thirty, your muscles are aching . . .

Everything I've done since—school, learning English, adjusting to other racial groups—those were easy adjustments. Because when you have a tough life, a rough physical life, you know, working, anything else you do later on is mediocre. All I have to do is look back at the old days, and just the thought of sweat coming down my forehead by nine o'clock, well, that makes it appear as if what I'm doing now is nothing compared to those days. Because when you start moving a twelve-foot ladder when you are about twelve years old for twelve hours a day, you can do just about anything else you want to do that you set your mind on. Now though, most kids around nowadays, they can make an easy buck . . .

It was probably in grade school, by sixth or seventh grade, that I decided I was going to go to college. You realize that if you don't want to work in the fields all your life, the only way you can do anything about it is to go to school and learn skills so you can better yourself—do something better than what your parents are doing. Because when I worked in the fields that many years, I only did it for one reason: to make a few bucks to go to school. I didn't do it because I liked to climb ladders. I didn't do it because I liked to sweat it out in the orchard when it was 100 degrees.

Quite a few kids from Locke went on to college. Quite a few didn't finish either. Some of them went to trade school . . . I went to Sacramento City College, then to Sacramento

The home of James S. Moser, Walnut Grove, 1986. Many Delta ranchers amassed *fortunes in agriculture with the help of nonunionized Chinese, Filipino, and Mexican labor. The Moser holdings include 3,500 acres planted to tomatoes, sugar beets, and pears throughout the Delta.*

State. I graduated with a degree in economics. My first job was with the [California] Department of Social Services. It's the only department I've ever worked for. Today I'm the interpreter—the translator coordinator for the Department of Social Services, state of California . . .

When you finish school, your education, you want to find employment for what you were trained for, or that is near to where you're going to live. So therefore, that's the main reason why I left the town of Locke. I mean, I still go down there several times a month to visit my mother, but I don't live there anymore because I want to live near where I work . . . I noticed that other people prior to me, when they got out of high school and went to school or even went to work, they left the town. So I knew that even before I got out of high school that probably when I made a living it would not be in the town of Locke. I knew I'd be leaving it, education-wise.

Because, you see, a career in ranching never came to my mind. Otherwise I would have majored in agricultural economics or something that had to do with agriculture. The only pepole who majored in those subjects were the sons of big ranchers down there, like Lincoln Chan's kids, or van Löben Sels, or the Grahams, or the Salisburys. Those kids, they went to UC Davis or San Luis Obispo, that had agricultural programs. They had it made. I mean, they get out of school, they just go back and start running the ranch. Whereas a guy—a Chinese kid out of Locke—what are their chances? I mean, all their parents were farm

laborers, and unless you're Lincoln Chan's kids [Lincoln Chan was one of the few Chinese farm laborers to become a successful landowner and rancher in the Delta] you go to college and major in agriculture, you come back and what are you going to do? You end up driving a tractor for someone else. In other words, the kids in the Delta whose parents were farmers and went on to college, they already had their future established for them. They had a future waiting for them when they graduated with a degree in agriculture. In my opinion, the kids in my generation that majored in agriculture in college, they were born with a golden spoon, more or less.

I'd say I've made a successful transition to

Delta farming in the 1980s. *After World War II, mechanization eliminated thousands of Delta farm labor jobs. Few sons and daughters of Locke's Chinese even sought farm work, however. Parents encouraged their children to go to college and achieve the standard of living the Golden Mountain had always promised.*

life here in Sacramento. My life here is fine. No problems, got good neighbors . . . It wasn't a real big adjustment, you know. In fact, I'd say the adjustment was easy because of the fact that the life I had at Locke and the adjustment that I had to make down there, any other transitions later on in life were easy.

But you know, I'd like to see something in the textbooks here about the Chinese history . . . because actually the Chinese have played a big part in California history. You go up to Marysville. That used to be one of the big Chinese communities up there, forty, fifty, sixty years ago. You go up there and see the Chinese shrines and all that. It's part of the original development of the town up there, and in some of the other gold mining towns too. What I'd like to see happen is a lot of these younger Chinese students to go on field trips and observe their ancestors' contribution towards the development of California. Because in my days, we didn't have things like that. In those days, the only thing I read in California history about the Chinese was the development of the railroad. And they wouldn't have more than two paragraphs—a page at the most.

Because the majority of the people in those days—even in part of my time—they were farm workers. And the farmers cannot survive without farm laborers. And that's what I'd like to see in the history books in regards to the Chinese and the Delta community: that when they first came over they really helped develop agriculture in the Sacramento Delta by supplying the labor force; and also, that the majority of them were able to maintain their Chinese heritage. And when they're able to read in history books about the type of work and the type of life that a person of my generation had to go through, I feel that they will appreciate it more than what they have now. And I'd also emphasize that the majority of the people in my generation, OK, we kept most of our so-called Chinese heritage.

Because now this generation, most of the kids today cannot speak their own language. And when they talk to somebody who can, they feel kind of embarrassed. I'd like to emphasize that learning a language is only a matter of wanting to learn. You can learn it. And you can maintain it and you can develop it. Because nowadays this generation, a lot of these kids, they don't . . . it's not that they can't learn the language—it's that they don't care. I'd definitely bring up my children to speak Chinese. There is a Chinese school here in Sacramento, down in Chinatown. And with a lot of the colleges and some of the high schools that have classes such as Black history or Asian history, I think they'll be able to appreciate the Chinese culture more . . .

As for Locke, it's just the old folks surviving there now, and as the years go by, there are fewer and fewer of the original ones there. Another ten years from now, there will be fewer Chinese there yet. There will probably be more Anglos moving in . . . it's being integrated. But in my opinion, it's something that the town itself can't control, because the younger generation when they get out of school, they leave. I certainly have no say or control over what happens to the town.

The only thing I hope is the type of people that moves in appreciates the character of the town, and hopefully continues the traditions and character of the town without destroying it. And from what I've seen, the people who have moved in there in the past ten years, they are the type of people that moved in there because they had an understanding of the situation of the town of Locke—that it's original. They probably took these features into consideration before they moved in and they are able to live along with it. They have not gone in there to make any changes. So even though the faces have changed in the last ten years, the town itself, overall, is still pretty close to the same.

陈
諫
靖

Connie Chan

Connie Chan was born in Hong Kong in 1963. She is the fifth of seven children, three of whom came to the United States with their mother in 1969. Bright, articulate, and thoroughly good-natured, Connie has dreams of being a doctor—although she's not sure whether these are her dreams or just her mother's. While serving as interpreter/translator of Bitter Melon *Connie was studying for her B.S. degree in Biological Sciences at the University of California at Davis, twenty-five miles from Locke. She was also working weekends as a saleswoman in a Davis shoestore, and summers as a check-out clerk at Ping Lee's Big Store in Walnut Grove. Connie's future holds a dilemma shared by other Chinese who have grown up in—and grown to love—the little town of Locke: how can she make it in the Golden Mountain, maintain her cultural identity as a Chinese, and also help preserve Locke's legacy.*

IT WAS VERY CROWDED in Hong Kong. The first thing I thought coming here was—wow, all the space!

But what I remember most was the feeling of being abandoned, because there were so few Chinese students who were going to Walnut Grove Elementary School then. There weren't many kids. In fact, I was the only Chinese there. At first I had a really tough time trying to get along with kids, because of the language barrier. I was forced to learn English, not like other immigrants from Mexico or Spanish-speaking kids, because of the barrier that was there. If I was going to do well and make

---

Mrs. Lon C. Owyoung (left) and Bitter Melon *translator Connie Chan, 1983.*
Mrs. Owyoung came to the United States to join her husband in 1950, at the age of fifty-three. She is eighty-six years old in this photograph. Connie Chan and Mrs. Owyoung are neighbors in Locke.

friends, it was clear I was going to have to get my tail in gear and learn English. I guess it wasn't really that tough a project, because I don't remember learning it at all . . .

My grandfather was originally over here. He was here from about 1920 on. He was in San Francisco for a while, and then came here and was working in Courtland with the Weaver family doing gardening work and farming for them. Then eventually he came down to Locke and spent the rest of his days here. When he was close to his eighties he sponsored us over here. It was my mom, my older sister, my younger brother, and I came over first. We came straight here. I have an aunt over in Hayward but we didn't stop there. We came straight here and my mom started work doing odd jobs like clearing out fields and weeding and stuff like that. She didn't know about the canneries until about two years later. She started working in the pear sheds in Walnut Grove. She got into the pear sheds and that's what she's been doing because of her English-speaking problems. I

***Mr. Soon Saer Choy, Connie Chan's
grandfather, 1974.*** *Mr. Soon came to the
United States in 1909 and worked as a Delta
farm laborer for more than fifty years, living
in Locke and the field labor barracks. In 1969
he sponsored the immigration of Connie's
family from Hong Kong. Mr. Soon lived with
the Chans on Key Street until his death in
1980, at the age of eighty-eight.*

came here when it was three days before my
sixth birthday.

My father is still back in Hong Kong. I
would rather not talk about that. But my other
brothers and sisters, I have one brother and
one sister who are both older than I am. They
have their own families. They are still in mainland China. They were left there because it was
hard for all of them to get out of China. My
father wanted my mom and two of my sisters to
go with my mom to Hong Kong, and my older
brother, because they were able to work and

support the family. I don't know exactly why my older sister was left over there. I've asked my mom a couple of times but she's been hesitant in telling me, so . . .

Over here, I was by myself most of the time, until the kids started to know me and I finally met some people and got involved in what they were doing. Once I got into fourth or fifth grade I finally got into the swing of things. I didn't feel isolated anymore. It was easier for me to try to excel, rather than just going along. In high school I played volleyball my first year. I was on the Asian Club, the California Scholastic Association, Spanish Club, the Year Book . . . my mom encouraged me to do whatever I wanted, though she had her expectations. I was supposed to learn English, for example. And by the time I was about eight, she expected me to do a lot of family business, take care of the family bills, because my older sister was ill and no one else was able to. Chinese are expected a lot to enter a professional field, like medicine. At one point I felt that she was heading me towards that. It's kind of a question now, whether I actually want to go into medicine, or whether it's family pressures I have going through my mind.

I'm the first one in my whole family to go through college—to even go through high school all the way. So there's an expectation . . . I have expectations of myself. The Chinese always have that family pressure, that you have to work hard and get somewhere. You talk to some Chinese businessmen and they will sit there and tell you that Chinese are hardworking people and they get somewhere no matter what they do. It's hard sometimes to have that expectation in the culture, and you're not able to live up to that expectation. It's hard for the family because there's that pride there. I'm expected to remember what my mom has gone through, what my family has gone through in China and here. And to use that knowledge as an incentive to further myself. I'm expected to remember my background, plus do well in

America. I think a lot of cultures do that . . .

I'll definitely teach my own children the [Chinese] language. I would tell them about their grandparents and what they've been through and about the culture. I really can't say if I would insist, make them go through a dual type of thing. On the other hand, I think I probably would, because I'm proud of my culture.

You know, I love it out here. It's really nice just to relax. But if you told me I had to stay here forever, years on end, I don't think I could do it. I don't want to say I don't *want* to live in Locke. But I know I could never stay here for the rest of my life, because there's so little exposure here to other areas. Maybe when I'm retired or something . . . I'm glad my mom is able to live here, though. And now the [state] government is trying to get in and fix everything. I was talking to her and she was telling me that it's so wonderful that they are finally going to fix the house, rewire the wiring and everything. But there's a lot of intrusions also.

It's hard for me to see what's going to happen here. The town was already very quiet when I got here [in 1969]. Mostly retired folks. I remember the older gentlemen used to give me little treats here and there. They treated us as grandchildren, all of them did. But you see how it is: as much as we may dislike it, they are going to all die off and a lot of the younger people aren't going to stay here. I don't think it's going to remain a Chinese town. I feel sad that it's going to die eventually. And I feel kind of angry at myself at times, because as one person I really can't do a lot in trying to maintain everything. It's really hard for me to say I won't be living here. I see this place in about twenty years or so as one big National Park area. They might rope off the areas where the houses are, but these grounds right here, the gardens, I really doubt they are going to stay for long. It's hard, because you are trying to let the modern, plus the old, be here. That's my opinion, anyway.

Carol Hall

何雄閂

The daughter of retired farm laborers Wai and Aida Hall, Carol Hall is one of only four or five Chinese-American adults under forty living in Locke today. She works odd jobs in and around Locke. Carol has left town several times for various pursuits in Sacramento, including waitressing and counter jobs, but caught between her desire to stay and save Locke and to leave and make a way for herself in the world, she still has not decided which way to go. Her ambivalence is only heightened by the ambiguous status of Locke today: will it be restored as a replica of itself, rebuilt as a commercial extravaganza, or simply allowed to slide into oblivion? Carol's father, referred to in this interview, died in September 1985. This interview was done by Todd Carrel as part of the work on his documentary film American Chinatown. *It is reprinted here with his permission.*

IT'S A VERY PRECIOUS TOWN, you know. God-awful precious. It's a place of peace, and whenever I go away for any length of time, I always come back to Locke. Chinese culture, they always want you to leave—to learn all about the world. I did that, but some way, somehow, I came back. I always come back here, where it's pure . . .

You know, like nobody cared about us before, when we were just little kids, playing. When we were just a little ghetto town. Now, all of a sudden everybody wants to cash in on us. You're in a little bottle and here's the rest of the world, you know, and everybody wants to break it. If people want to make money, that's fine and well. Just give us a fair chance. Because the old folks, this is their place until they die, their place of peace. They pretty much keep out of things; they just watch. They've learned how to adjust, and they keep their own little world.

But in twenty years it won't be Locke any more, as it stands. It's sad knowing that. One gentleman on a bench, then all of a sudden there's five, then you see three, two, one . . .

All the old men that used to live in back of Locke, I used to run and talk to them, and we laughed. Now, just watching each one go, one by one—you want to make me cry, don't you? You know my father's one of them too. Soon they're all going to be gone. And then I wonder what. If only the kids would all come back. But when they get away to college they always return for a short while, and go back out. It gets to the point—with me it gets so intense, I just want to run away. I just want to go too. But somehow I'm hanging in there.

Carol Hall, Main Steet, 1976.

Afterword

Ow Hoy Kee   *Ng So Yung*
Jone Ho Leong   *Suen Hoon Sum*
Wong Yow   *Bing Fai Chow*
Jo Lung   *Tommy J. King*

As you wind down River Road, the big sign lures you off the highway: "Welcome to Locke." You nose your car off the levee and find Main Street looking much as it did when the cover photo was taken in 1976—a little more faded, a little more precarious, a little more forlorn, but still there. Over its nearly ninety-year history, Locke has withstood the threat of fire and floods, the pain of poverty, discrimination, and neglect, and almost total abandonment by its original Chinese residents and their offspring. But at the beginning of the twenty-first century, this tiny enclave now faces perhaps its greatest challenge—legitimate self-government.

In a surprising development, the Sacramento County Housing and Redevelopment Agency (SHRA) recently purchased the ten-acre town site as the first step in restoring Locke and eventually transferring ownership of the land to its residents for the first time in history. The catch is, this proudly anarchistic haven must now establish a governing body that operates under the rules and regulations of the county, state, and federal governments—entities the townspeople of Locke have never had much desire or need to deal with. Against all odds, it appears that Locke is going to survive to see its one hundredth anniversary in 2015. The major question is: survive as what?

America's last rural all-Chinese town ceased being an all-Chinese town in the 1970s. That Locke remained all-Chinese for as long as it did says as much about the extraordinary isolation and insularity of the Chinese-American experience as anything else. Locke filled a need for people spurned, exploited, and misunderstood by the surrounding Anglo culture. "When they built the town, they thought they were only going to be there five, six, ten years at the most and then get the heck out," recalls Ping Lee, now 84. "They just wanted a roof over their head, make their money, and go back to where they were wanted—to China." But as the stories of *Bitter Melon* make clear, revolution and war in China, poverty and discrimination in America, and the numbing cycles of farm labor conspired to hold generations of Chinese in Locke. Here they became Chinese-*Americans*—some eagerly, by choice, and others reluctantly, by default. Here they helped establish a town so unique that in 1990 it was designated a national historic landmark.

Several plans to "save" Locke have surfaced over the past thirty years, including one in 1977 by the same Sacramento Housing and Redevelopment Agency. In the midst of their planning, however, Hong Kong developer Ng Tor Tai bought the town and 490 surrounding acres for $700,000. This extraordinary purchase was made possible by the 1913 Alien Land Act, repealed in 1952, which forbade Chinese people and others ineligible for citizenship from owning land in America; despite several efforts, the people of Locke had never been able to buy the land themselves. Ironically, it was a Chinese developer living in Hong Kong who eventually bought the whole package.

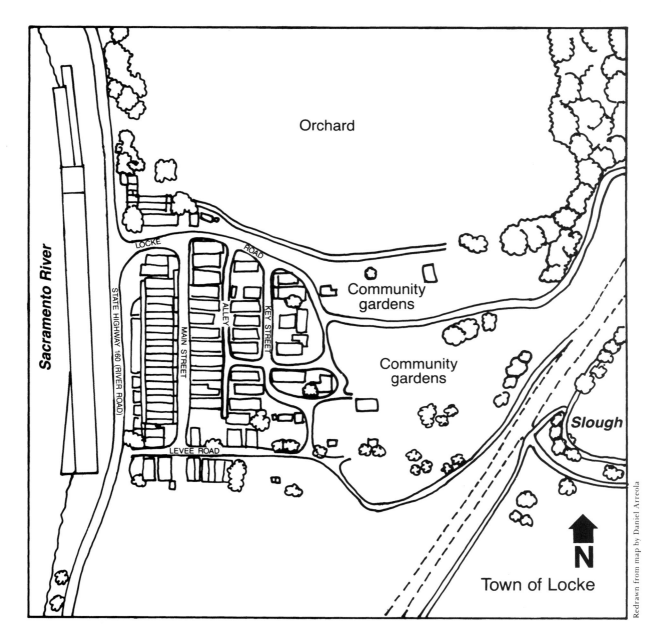

Redrawn from map by Daniel Arreola

Sacramento River

State Highway 160 (River Road)

Orchard

LOCKE ROAD

MAIN STREET

ALLEY

KEY STREET

LEVEE ROAD

Community gardens

Community gardens

Slough

N

Town of Locke

Ng Tor Tai's hopes to preserve Locke's cultural heritage while constructing luxury homes behind the town never went through, but the county continued to be concerned with the town's survival and established a Special Planning Area in 1979 to forestall incongruous development. Unfortunately, the town's bizarre ownership scheme has forestalled *any* kind of development in Locke. Public agencies cannot fund projects where a single property owner controls the whole town, while private lenders refuse to finance projects where a building owner doesn't own the deed of trust to his land.

Caught in this bureaucratic twilight zone, Locke began to wither away. Many of its Chinese residents already had left for universities, professional schools, jobs, and marriages in the fast-growing suburbs of California. Of the eighty or so residents in Locke today, only ten are Chinese. The rest are an eclectic group of whites, Mexicans, and Filipinos, artists and retirees, carpenters, farmworkers, and jacks-of-all-trades. Many of Locke's storefronts and clapboard homes have fallen into disrepair. The old Star Theater, which once housed Chinese opera troupes touring America, sags at its center like a fat man searching for a chair. The town's infrastructure—sewers, streets, sidewalks, lights—is decaying as well.

In 1999, Locke's owners were warned by state water officials that if its antiquated sewer system weren't fixed, the town might have to be vacated. The cost of the upgrade—one million dollars—was beyond Locke Property Development's ability to pay. Public funds were available to help but could not be spent to benefit Locke's single landowner. Once again, the SHRA stepped forward. It offered to purchase the ten acres beneath the town and help secure a grant from the U.S. Department of Agriculture to fix the sewer system. A formula to subdivide Locke's properties would then be worked out and the land beneath the buildings sold to individual owners for the first time in history. The plan was driven by SHRA staff and county leadership, including Sacramento County Supervisor Don Nottoli. "Locke has such a unique story," says Nottoli, who has pushed to save the town. "It's such a strong part of the history of the Delta and development of California."

Clarence Chu, owner and general manager of Locke Property Development, was overjoyed. Caught for years between the town's absentee owner and Locke's mostly low-income residents, Chu had tried to keep land rents, fees, and expenditures to a minimum. It was a strategy that met the short-term needs of the owner and residents but seriously hampered the town's ability to improve itself. "The town was dying," says Mr. Chu, brother-in-law to Ng Tor Tai. "This will break the deadlock. People in the town will have a deed of trust to their land, and new owners will hopefully be drawn in who can help revitalize the town."

Locke Property Development agreed to sell the land beneath the town to SHRA for $250,000. When escrow closes it will end a series of transactions that began in 1915 with a handshake between local landowner George Locke and Chinese immigrants searching for a home. As the new owner, SHRA will manage Locke until the town's property is subdivided into individual parcels and sold to the building owners. Toward that end, a seventeen-member Citizens Advisory Committee (CAC) has been appointed, made up of Locke residents, merchants, and former residents, members of Chinese-American historical and cultural organizations, and representatives of interested government agencies.

The first meeting of the Locke Citizens Advisory Committee took place September 25, 2001, in the auditorium of Walnut Grove's Jean Harvey School (ironically, the site of the all-white school from which Locke's residents were excluded until 1941). It was the first meeting ever of an officially recognized governing body for the town—Locke was run for its first sixty years by a self-selected group of merchants, and it has been run since 1978 by Locke Property Development. The CAC sketched out the tasks ahead, including practical matters that the townspeople want to work on immediately— street and sidewalk maintenance, sprinklers and fire protection, storm drainage, and leash laws. "First things first," says Clarence Chu. "Let's get the sewer in, then within the next two years help us subdivide so everyone can have their own property deed. We've had enough of people's dreams." Connie King, the *de facto* manager of Locke prior to 1978, agrees. Her priorities are streetlights, restrooms for tourists, a playground for the town's children, and, most important, holding the lease to the land under her home.

While everyone on the CAC agrees that Locke's unique character should be preserved, exactly how is up for grabs. "What era do we preserve, and how deeply do we get into it?" one CAC representative asked. Some want dragonboat races on the slough behind town, something that has never happened there. Others want a

Chinese opera to perform, which did happen, regularly, in the 1920s. Some want to guard against "Orientalism"—pagodas and tacky T-shirt shops—and feature only authentic historical exhibits. But would that include reproductions of the town's whorehouses, speakeasies, and opium dens? Most support a museum commemorating Locke's contributions to the economic and cultural development of the Delta. "I want people coming to Locke to be inspired by our history and feel a connection with the people who were here before," Clarence Chu says enthusiastically.

Clarence Chu's other dream is to revive the once-vital businesses on Main Street. Some of the ideas that have been proposed are a tea house, a bed-and-breakfast, additional stores and restaurants, and a "cultural village" centered on Main Street, with practitioners of Chinese calligraphy, painting, music, and crafts. Some in town don't want that much change. "People who move here for the rural atmosphere and then complain that it lacks amenities forget what it is that attracted them in the first place," says Ronnie Maiden, a sixteen-year resident of Locke who has raised three children here. "I don't want business concerns to outweigh the concerns of the residents who make this a living town."

The CAC's task is complicated by the fact that Locke is no longer an all-Chinese town. Eight members of the CAC are Chinese; only four, plus an alternate, are Locke residents. As one CAC member commented, "There is a broader array of interests in what happens to Locke than just the people who live there." One of those interests is the Chinese-American nonprofit community. "Locke is the most important thing happening in Asian America today," says Christina Fa, one of two representatives on the CAC from the Chinese-American Council of Sacramento. To date, Asian-American groups have been conspicuously absent in Locke's affairs. Apparently that's about to change. "It's incredibly important symbolically for these people to be given the chance to own that land," Christina Fa believes. "If we [the Chinese community] don't do our part to revitalize Locke, it will be written out of history."

After two uneventful meetings of the CAC, a third erupted into chaos. One Chinese resident, born and raised in the town, was irate that the county planned to charge a price for land that some families had been paying rent on for fifty years or more. The cost of subdividing Locke could be thousands of dollars above the cost of the actual land itself—which SHRA estimated at between four and five thousand dollars per parcel. Another fear expressed was that California State Parks might take over the town and subject residents to what one merchant described as "polyester-coated park rangers running up and down Main Street telling us we can't be out after nine." To address that fear, Locke Property Development insisted that the sales contract for the town specify that the land be subdivided and sold to the building owners. This will ensure that while the state parks department and other government agencies may become property owners in the town, no one will ever again be *the* owner.

But the biggest fear is that nothing will happen at all. "We've been going through this for so long," Connie King laments. "They came and took our pictures, everything was going to change [under SHRA's 1977 plan]. We've been talking about this for forty years now." Most official parties believe that the plan will go ahead: the county's purchase of the town should be completed early in 2002; State Parks wants to help—not smother—the town; and for the first time, Chinese-American groups are taking an active interest in the preservation of Locke.

But can Locke govern itself? Will the seventeen disparate members of the CAC be able to negotiate complex issues like land subdivision, historical preservation, and economic development while managing everyday concerns such as assessment districts, fire prevention, and public parking? "Yes," believes SHRA consultant Seann Rooney. "I think they'll have no problem raising money, there's so much interest in this town." Then he added more warily, "It's probably more complicated than anyone thought it was going to be."

A town of just eighty people, Locke may turn out to be as difficult to govern as New York City, where fifty-one city council members are elected to represent their slice of America's largest metropolis. In Locke, all eighty people must be heard. And before the town goes forward, it seems as if the thousands of men and women who labored for a dollar a day and died without ever owning a piece of Golden Mountain must be heard as well.

"When I walk the streets of Locke in the morning and the tule fog is just lifting off the slough, I can feel the spirits of all the people who lived there," says Sharon Boldt, owner of the River Road Gallery on Main Street and a member of the CAC. "I see the Chinese people walking down the streets. I see the ladies in the garden with their hats on. You can still feel their spirit of industry and hard work and inspiration, and I'd like to see that feeling preserved."

By all appearances, this is the best and perhaps last opportunity to save Locke. The government that for so long oppressed the people of Locke and then for decades ignored them has turned the tables and handed the town back to them to decide its fate. What Locke looks like on its hundredth anniversary now rests in the hands of seventeen people who claim to have the town's best interests—past, present, and future—in their hearts. We wish them every success in their historic task.

Connie King in her garden, Locke, 2001. *Born in Isleton in 1923, Constance Tom married Tommy J. King and moved to Locke in 1949. Gracious and surprisingly strong-willed, Connie King has been the force that kept Locke together for years. "We ran the town," Ping Lee says about the unofficial council that governed Locke, "but Connie did all the work." For decades she collected ground rents for Clay Locke, and water and garbage fees for the town. Every Sunday at noon she tested the town's siren—people set their watches by it. She raised two children and attended to her husband, who died in 1997 after a long illness, and helped run the River Road Art Gallery. She's loaned money, dispensed advice, mediated disputes, and helped people give birth and bury the dead. "I married a man who was raised here," she says. "But I also married a town." In May 2001, with Sacramento County's board of supervisors ready to vote on whether to help preserve the town, supporters urged their reluctant "Locke Mom" to speak. "I'm here to represent the men who have gone," she began, opening a bit of the town's collective memory stored in her heart. "I want to see the town preserved in memory of the Chinese who built the railroads, who built the levees, who planted all the pear trees up and down the Delta, who built the town of Locke. I promised those men we would own the land under our homes one day. We've been waiting a long time for this."*

Appendix I

Chinese Immigration and Settlement

CONDITIONS IN NINETEENTH-CENTURY CHINA

Between 1840 and 1900, 2.5 million Chinese left China for Southeast Asia, Latin America, Australia, and the United States, fleeing a series of catastrophes that shook their four thousand-year-old civilization to its foundations. It was a period of domestic insurrections and civil war, foreign bombardment, invasions, and natural cataclysms of unparalleled severity—floods, earthquakes, fires, and drought. This period also saw unprecedented population increases throughout China: between 1802 and 1834, Chinese census figures indicate an estimated increase in population of *100 million* people, pushing the total population of the Chinese Empire to better than 400 million by 1840. These chaotic conditions rendered China extremely vulnerable to British, French, Russian, and Japanese designs on her lands; but the West's interventions in Chinese affairs only hastened the decline of the Celestial Empire, and, ironically, the migration of millions of Chinese to western countries.

COLLAPSE OF A FOUR-THOUSAND-YEAR-OLD EMPIRE

1838	Beginning of the Great Recession, leading to devaluation of Chinese currency and 100-year destabilization of its economy
1840	British attack on Ning-po in southern China, beginning the First Opium War (the British were defending the right to import opium to China from their colonies in India)
1842	British annex Hong Kong
1856	Second Opium War: British bombard Canton, annex Kowloon
1851–1864	T'ai Ping Rebellion: 20–30 million killed in civil war
1871	Russians occupy the Ili territory of China
1874	Japanese attack Formosa
1884	French bombard Fuzhou, blockade Shanghai and Beijing
1887	Portuguese annex Macao, exact huge reparations from China
1895	Japan annexes Taiwan, exacts reparations
1896–1902	Germany, Russia, France, Japan, Great Britain, Belgium, Italy, and Austria exact crippling concessions and reparations from the tottering Chinese government. Unsuccessful Boxer Rebellion leads to further disintegration
1911	Manchu Dynasty overthrown. First Republican government in Chinese history established

Hardest hit by invasions, economic recession, and overpopulation were China's southeastern provinces of Guangdong and Fujian, where the Pearl River Delta meets the South China Sea. Dominated by the port cities of Guangzhou (Canton), Macao, and Hong Kong, this region was the only entry point for the western powers into China between 1757 and 1840. It was also the site of many important—and destructive—battles between China and the West, and the jumping off point for millions of Chinese peasants who left dreaming of a better life in *Gum Shan*—the Gold Mountain of California—or elsewhere in the New World. Until World War II, when American immigration laws for Chinese were relaxed, more than 80 percent of Chinese immigrants came from Guangdong Province.

CHINESE IN THE UNITED STATES

Driven from their homelands by economic recession and political turmoil, millions fled China to destinations overseas, including silver mines in Peru and sugar cane plantations in Cuba. By 1870, the Chinese were the largest single ethnic group working the California goldfields, mining mostly abandoned claims in teams for self-protection. Over half of the miners in Oregon and Idaho (silver, lead, bauxite) at this time were Chinese, as were a quarter of the miners in Washington Territory.

Prior to passage of the Chinese Exclusion Act, Chinese made up one-fifth of all human labor in California: 90 percent of the workforce on the Central Pacific Railroad, the majority of the state's farm laborers, and most of the labor force constructing the levee system of the Sacramento–San Joaquin Delta. According to California wine historian William Heinz, the Chinese made up 80 percent of California's wine-industry labor force in the nineteenth century. Chinese fishing villages also dotted the coast from Baja California to the Oregon border.

Without passage of the Chinese Exclusion Act in 1882, there seems little doubt that Chinese today would constitute one of America's most numerous and influential ethnic groups. While the 1965 Immigration Act put Chinese immigrants on an equal par with other nationalities, nearly a century of official discrimination has had its effect. In 1980, the official United States Census showed the Chinese population at slightly more than 800,000—an estimated .36 percent of the country's total.

CHINESE IN THE UNITED STATES, 1850–1980

1850	4,825	1920	61,639
1860	34,933	1930	74,954
1870	63,199	1940	77,504
1880	105,465	1950	117,629
1882	132,300	1960	198,958
1890	107,488	1970	435,062
1900	89,863	1980	812,178
1910	71,531		

Sources: Chinese Historical Society of America
Census Population, U.S. Department of
Commerce

Appendix II

A Chinese Town on the Sacramento   BY ESTHER A. THOMAS

Kagawa found his workshop for the refining of human nature and the testing of his own consecration in the slums of Japan. Muriel Lester and Hugh Redwood had their souls tried among the destitute of England. Albert Schweitzer buried himself with God in the moral blackness of an African town.

One sings the praises of these devoted followers of Jesus Christ and recognizes the humble spots which they glorified, yet there are self-sacrificing individuals working in obscure slums the world over, about whom one seldom hears. They go on patiently bringing into unwholesome localities a permeating influence that creeps like a sunbeam into dark crevices and corners some of which are not on maps.

One such community, where vice and degradation are disgustingly apparent, is a town called Locke, situated in the delta region of the Sacramento River, twenty-five miles south of the capital of California. Locke is a Chinese village, half a mile square, with a population of about six hundred. There are only thirty-one Christians in the town.

The village was established in 1915, when a fire destroyed the Chinatown of Walnut Grove, another town on the river bank. Fleeing Chinese men and women stopped at an uninhabited location and there built their homes. A general store was erected on the levee, and a number of dwelling houses, poor in construction and material, soon followed. The unpaved streets are nothing more than alleys ten to fourteen feet in width. Immediately after the homes were ready for occupancy, there came gambling houses and brothels.

Every known kind of gambling goes on in this small town, practically all of it being illegal. Raids are made periodically but a code of warning signals exists between friends of the gamblers and the people in Locke, so that when the officers arrive the dens are closed and the men are innocently pitching "horse-shoes" in the alleys. Even the Chinese women maintain gambling clubs and spend their money in lottery games and Mah Jung. Well dressed white men and women from adjoining towns are occasionally seen in the gambling houses of Locke.

The tiny village, of not more than sixty-five houses, harbors eight brothels in which are found only white women. These girls are victims of white slave masters and as soon as one of the women dies or goes away, it is an easy matter to put another in her place. Chinese, Japanese and Filipino men patronize these brothels. At present there is only one respectable white woman in Locke and she is the missionary at the Christian Center. It is not safe for her to be out on the roads alone at night.

One of the best arguments in favor of the whole-hearted continuance of foreign missions has been proved at Locke. Into this unattractive environment, made ugly by the viciousness of human degradation, came Jesus Christ, through the personality of Mrs. Ong Yip, a graduate of a Christian Mission School in Hong Kong. This consecrated Chinese woman came from the Orient to bring to America what she had learned there from American missionaries. With no equipment, Mrs. Yip began the only Christian work in the area, consisting of Sunday school classes for children and religious services for adults. Her "auditorium" was the corner of a laundry building.

In 1919, Dr. Charles R. Shepherd, Director of Chinese Missions for the American Baptist Home Mission Society, being greatly impressed by the work, made arrangements to rent more suitable quarters and the school grew so rapidly that it was soon necessary to secure another location. In

Reprinted from *The Missionary Review of the World,* vol. 57, 1934.

1922 a building, known as the Locke Christian Center, was erected and later a missionary was appointed by the Woman's American Baptist Home Mission Society to superintend the work.

Girls were gathered into Sunday school classes and clubs where they were taught music, sewing and principles of cleanliness. In the beginning it was difficult to interest the boys in the activities of the Christian Center. Up to three years ago only four boys regularly attended the Mission. In 1929 the Chinese leaders developed a sudden antagonism to the Center and its workers and protested against the Christian influence by opening a joss house. The attendants brought out a ceremonial lion of wood, paper and silk and paraded with it through the alleys of the village. Chinese brothel women from another town, dressed in red satin with gold braid trimmings, walked in the rear of the procession. This demonstration made a profound impression upon the boys and the work of winning them had to be started over again. Today, however, there are thirty-five boys in regular attendance at the Mission.

Nearly all of the Chinese mothers in Locke work in the canneries while their children play in the dirty alleys. On the adjoining ranches women do the plowing, often with tiny babies strapped to their backs. On one ranch the missionary found a man with two wives, each with a large family, and all of them living in poverty and filth, in close proximity to sixty hogs whose abode was scarcely less inviting. In another ranch house, in a room the temperature of which registered ninety-eight degrees, a baby was found wrapped in four layers of men's woolen suiting. The child was covered with sores and it took months of care to bring it to normalcy. As soon as the missionaries had won the confidence of the women, mothers' classes were formed and little by little they have come to realize the healing value of nursing and American medicines. Today the Public Health nurse reports the Chinese children under the care of the Christian Center at Locke the healthiest along the river.

The men of this town have caused much annoyance to the Christian workers, not only because of their indifference to the influence of the Center, but because of their sometimes sudden, and often strenuous, antagonism. The missionaries, however, with gentle strategy, have captured their interest by offering an opportunity to learn English. The younger men have not hesitated to avail themselves of the chance to study at the Center, and, with a growing sense of devotion, now carry on their own worship service.

There is no other town in the world quite like Locke with its wide-open gambling, white women prostitutes, heathen joss houses, women hitched to plows, open polygamy, animal and human filth in abundance and over it all the calm, persistent influence of a Christian Center dedicated to the lifting of humanity Godward. Little by little the sunbeam of Christianity is purifying and making beautiful the sordid spots.

A slum is a low or squalid neighborhood consisting of a slovenly or vicious population, or it is the laboratory where human degradation can be transformed through an "Inasmuch" challenge, and where human souls can be refined through a "Whosoever" invitation.

Bibliography

American Chinatown, a 30-minute documentary film on the people of Locke and the plight of their community, by Todd Carrel, copyright 1981. Distributed for educational use by University of California Extension Media Center, 2176 Shattuck Ave., Berkeley, CA 94704, (510) 642–0460.

Arreola, Daniel. "Locke, California: Persistence and Change in the Cultural Landscape of a Delta Chinatown." Master's thesis, California State University, Hayward (1975).

Barth, Gunther. *Bitter Strength: A History of the Chinese in America, 1850–1870.* Cambridge, MA: Harvard University Press, 1964.

Chinn, Thomas W., ed., Him Mark Lai and Philip P. Choy, assoc. eds. *A History of the Chinese in California: A Syllabus.* San Francisco: Chinese Historical Society of America, 1969.

Chu, George. "Chinatowns in the Delta: The Chinese in the Sacramento and San Joaquin Delta, 1870–1960." *California Historical Quarterly* 49, no. 1 (March 1970): 21–37.

Francis, Lura. "The Historic Delta." *Pacific Historian* 23 (1979): 45–57..

Gernet, Jacques. *A History of Chinese Civilization.* Cambridge: Cambridge University Press, 1982.

Goto, Leo, ed. *A Plan and Action Program for Locke.* Sacramento: Sacramento Housing & Redevelopment Agency, 1977.

Graham, Kathleen, ed. *The Sacramento River Delta.* Walnut Grove, CA: Sacramento River Delta Historical Society, 1982.

Hoexter, Corrine K. *From Canton to California: The Epic of Chinese Immigration.* New York: Four Winds Press, 1976.

Kagiwada, George. "Report on Locke: A Historical Overview and Call for Action." *AmerAsia* 9, no. 2 (1982):57–78.

Kingston, Maxine H. *China Men.* New York: Ballantine, 1980.

Knoll, Tricia. *Becoming Americans: Asian Sojourners, Immigrants, and Refugees in the Western United States.* Portland, OR: Coast to Coast Books, 1982.

Lai, H. M., and Choy, Philip P. *Outlines: History of the Chinese in America.* San Francisco, 1973.

Lee, John, ed. *The Golden Mountain: Chinese Tales Told in California.* Washington, D.C.: WPA Project No. 665–08–3–236.

Leung, Peter C. Y. *One Day, One Dollar: Locke, California, and the Chinese Farming Experience in the Sacramento Delta.* El Cerrito, CA: Chinese/Chinese American History Project, 1984.

McCunn, Ruthanne Lum. *An Illustrated History of the Chinese in America.* San Francisco: Design Enterprises, 1979.

Nee, Victor, and Brett de Bary. *Long Time Californ': A Documentary Study of an American Chinatown.* New York: Patheon Books, 1972.

Rossi, Jean. "Lee Bing, Founder of California Historical Town of Locke." *Pacific Historian* 20, no. 4 (Winter 1976): 351–66.

Thernstrom, Stephen, ed. *Harvard Encyclopedia of American Ethnic Groups.* Cambridge, MA: Harvard University Press, 1980.

Thomas, Esther A. "A Chinese Town on the Sacramento." *Missionary Review of the World* 57 (1934): 407–8.

Trillin, Calvin. "U.S. Journal: Locke, Calif., the Last Chinatown." *The New Yorker* 54, no. 1 (February 20, 1978): 109–13.

Tung, W. L. *The Chinese in America, 1820–1973: A Chronology & Fact Book.* Dobbs Ferry, NY: Oceana, 1974.

Yee, Mrs. Dale. "Remembering 'Tai Han' or 'Lockee.'" *East/West Chinese American Journal,* February 19, 1975, p. 8.

Yip, Christopher. "Locke, California, and the Chinese-Americans." Master's thesis, University of California, Berkeley, 1977.

HEYDAY INSTITUTE

Since its founding in 1974, Heyday Books has occupied a unique niche in the publishing world, specializing in books that foster an understanding of the history, literature, art, environment, social issues, and culture of California and the West. We are a 501(c)(3) nonprofit organization based in Berkeley, California, serving a wide range of people and audiences.

We are grateful for the generous funding we've received for our publications and programs during the past year from foundations and more than 300 individual donors. Major supporters include:

Anonymous; Anthony Andreas, Jr., Audubon, Barnes & Noble bookstores; Bay Tree Fund; S.D. Bechtel, Jr. Foundation; California Council for the Humanities; California Oak Foundation; Candelaria Fund; Columbia Foundation; Colusa Indian Community Council; Federated Indians of Graton Rancheria; Wallace Alexander Gerbode Foundation; Richard & Rhoda Goldman Fund; Evelyn & Walter Haas, Jr. Fund; Walter & Elise Haas Fund; Hopland Band of Pomo Indians; James Irvine Foundation; George Frederick Jewett Foundation; LEF Foundation; David Mas Masumoto; Michael McCone; Middletown Rancheria Tribal Council; Gordon & Betty Moore Foundation; Morongo Band of Mission Indians; National Endowment for the Arts; National Park Service; Poets & Writers; Rim of the World Interpretive Association; River Rock Casino; Alan Rosenus; San Francisco Foundation; John-Austin Saviano/Moore Foundation; Sandy Cold Shapero; Ernest & June Siva; L.J. Skaggs and Mary C. Skaggs Foundation; Swinerton Family Fund; Victorian Alliance; Susan Swig Watkins; and the Harold & Alma White Memorial Fund.

For more information about Heyday Institute, our publications and programs,
please visit our website at www.heydaybooks.com.